Advance Praise
for *Seeing the Son of God*

Merlin Merritt has spent much of his life exploring two worlds—the world of space and the world of Scripture. As a NASA engineer, he helped people get to the moon. As a longtime Bible study teacher and minister of education at a church, he helped people understand the Bible. In this book, those two worlds intersect, and we get to explore both of those worlds with him. It's a delightful and illuminating adventure.

—Judson Edwards
Author of *Quiet Faith* and *Bugles in the Afternoon*

This book is an exhilarating story that takes readers behind the scenes during the events of the *Apollo 13* mission. Through his engaging illustration of the numerous catastrophic events during the mission, he provides readers with little-known spiritual revelations he and others perceived, which would ultimately transform all the lives that bore witness to it. Building on this experience, he expertly weaves together the writings of well-respected scientists and theologians to present astute arguments for several controversial issues that have been sources of intense debate. He does so, however, in a loving manner that speaks to both scientist and theologian alike and prompts the reader to consider that the search for truth is not complete without the consideration of both.

—K. Leigh Greathouse
Assistant Professor, Nutrition Sciences
Baylor University, Waco, Texas

Scientific discoveries at times have challenged believers who see a tension between their Christian faith and science. It is with pleasure that I read Walter Merlin Merritt's account of how he has integrated his experiences as a NASA engineer with his deep faith. I was encouraged by the honesty and the charity of his account.

—Jeffrey Green
Associate Professor of Philosophy
Houston Baptist University

Merlin Merritt is one of the finest and most sincere people I had the privilege of getting to know while working on my book. As instrumental as he and other flight controllers were in bringing the crew of *Apollo 13* home safely, Merlin has exhibited that same kind of passionate intensity in his own book in which he examines the relationship between science and faith. You won't be able to put it down!

—Rick Houston
Author of *Go, Flight: The Unsung Heroes of Mission Control*

A captivating, thoughtful, honest, heartwarming, and insightful read on a timely and timeless subject. *Seeing the Son on the Way to the Moon* will stimulate your mind, stir your heart, and increase your faith. Merritt offers a fascinating account of the often breathtaking experiences, personal emotions, and candid faith-struggles involved in the early NASA space program. He also provides practical and biblically based observations and answers to one of life's toughest faith-questions, "How can faith and science intersect and help each other?"

—Bill Nichols
Professor of Philosophy and Pastor/Counselor
Author of *Healthy Faith: A Strategic Lifestyle Plan to Transform Your Head, Heart, and Hands*

W. Merlin Merritt

SEEING THE SON ON THE WAY TO THE MOON

A NASA Engineer's Reflection on Science and Faith

Smyth & Helwys Publishing, Inc.
6316 Peake Road
Macon, Georgia 31210-3960
1-800-747-3016
©2018 by Walter Merlin Merritt
All rights reserved.

Library of Congress Cataloging-in-Publication Data

Names: Merritt, Walter Merlin, author.
Title: Seeing the Son on the way to the moon : a NASA engineer's reflection
on science and faith / by Walter Merlin Merritt.
Description: Macon : Smyth & Helwys, 2018. | Includes bibliographical
references.
Identifiers: LCCN 2017053170 | ISBN 9781573129930 (pbk. : alk. paper)
Subjects: LCSH: Religion and science. | Christianity and astronautics. |
Apologetics. | Merritt, Walter Merlin--Religion.
Classification: LCC BL254 .M47 2018 | DDC 261.5/5--dc23
LC record available at https://lccn.loc.gov/2017053170

Disclaimer of Liability: With respect to statements of opinion or fact available in this work of nonfiction, Smyth & Helwys Publishing Inc. nor any of its employees, makes any warranty, express or implied, or assumes any legal liability or responsibility for the accuracy or completeness of any information disclosed, or represents that its use would not infringe privately-owned rights.

To my loving wife, Shirley,

My children, Michael and Julie, and

my grandchildren, Evelyn, Travis, Huck, August, Sophia, and Sage

Acknowledgment

I would like to thank my niece, Angela Raley,
for her extensive work in editing this book.

Contents

Introduction   1

Chapter 1: **The Race to the Moon**   5

Chapter 2: **Apollo–Landing on the Moon**   17

Chapter 3: *Apollo 13*–**The Rest of the Story**   31

Chapter 4: **Sensing Spiritual Realities in a Physical World**   47

Chapter 5: **The Witness from Cosmology**   59

Chapter 6: **Origins**   71

Chapter 7: **Intersection of Faith and Science**   83

Chapter 8: **Seeing the Son, Knowing the Father**   99

Introduction

This book not only chronicles my experiences and emotions regarding the early NASA space program but also reflects my struggles to integrate faith and science in the real world. One might even question whether it is possible to bring together faith and science in any kind of congruent worldview since the methods of measurement, language, and experiences are so different. Are we talking apples and oranges here? Or, at some deeper level, are there themes and truths in both disciplines that interact and speak to each other?

I believe the issue of faith and science is an important topic because people are asking honest questions and long to make sense of things, and of course many of these issues affect their worldview and resultant lifestyle. There are several points of intersection between science and Christian theology that many people perceive as areas of conflict. They reason that if science says the world and the universe were created some 14 billion years ago through evolutionary means and seems to conflict with the biblical account of creation, then how can we believe in the rest? Many fundamentalists and evangelicals say that if you are an orthodox Christian with a high view of the Bible, you can't really believe in any form of evolution. Many atheists and agnostics argue that if you believe in science and evolution, you can't believe in God. Others have difficulty accepting miraculous events as presented in the Bible. Many believers see the technological and medical advances achieved through science as beneficial and have a positive view of science, but they have trouble reconciling what science seems to tell them about evolution, the age of the Earth, and their traditional theological beliefs. Therefore, these apparent paradoxes can result in strong opposing views about science and the Christian faith, which sometimes lead to tension and confusion.

In recent years, scientists and theologians have published a number of outstanding books on the subject of science and faith. Such books include *One World—The Interaction of Science and Theology* and *Exploring Reality: The Intertwining of Science and Religion* by John Polkinghorne; *God and the New Physics* by Paul Davies; *Romancing the Universe* by Jeffery Sobosan; and *The Language of God* by Francis Collins. As someone trained in engineering, science, and theology, and also having experienced firsthand the difficulties and discoveries of the early space program, I simply add my views to harmonize the interaction of science and faith. After studying and experiencing the changes in scientific thought of the past fifty years and getting a fresh perspective on biblical interpretations, I believe science and the Christian faith not only can be harmonized but also have a lot to say to each other. My faith component compels me to describe both my own experiences of how faith and science interact as well as their implications for the future. I agree with John Polkinghorne, who is a physicist, Catholic priest, and a former professor at Cambridge University, and says there must be no compartmentalization between theology and science; they must be held together by and in the Creator, who is the single reality of all there is.[1] Science and theology both pursue truth.

One of my favorite quotes is from Albert Einstein, who said, "Religion without science is blind, and science without religion is lame."[2] In other words, religion or faith can't see far without help, and science is an important window that gives us insight and vision into the spiritual world. Are you blind in your religion? Have you looked at the stars lately? Have you looked at the natural world and marveled at its construction? Our Sun belongs to the Milky Way, a cluster of some 200 billion stars shaped like a giant spiral. The Sun, located in one of the arms, completes one turn every 250 million years. To avoid awkward large numbers, most astronomers use the light-year as a form of measurement. A light-year is the distance it takes light to travel in one year at 186,000 miles per second. The average size of a galaxy is 100,000 light-years across, and the average distance between galaxies is 3 million light-years. Our nearest galactic neighbor, the Andromeda Galaxy, is 2 million light-years away. As we marvel at the grandeur of the universe, some of us cannot help wondering at the possibility of a divine being.

The second part of Einstein's statement, "science without religion is lame," is also true. In other words, it is incomplete, flat— it lacks true life. Theology takes our ability to comprehend the rational universe and sees in it a deeper truth at the heart of the cosmos; our faith interprets what science is finding. Both theology and our faith aim to bring answers to the questions posed by science.

Theology and the realities of the Christian faith for the twenty-first century must depend not only on philosophy to shape its dimensions but also on scientific truths to bring depth and new perspectives to its reality. As Jeffrey Sobosan writes, "Christianity no longer can assume that the primary intellectual trait of the culture in which it exists is philosophy."[3] That is, Christian apologetics must use philosophical pursuits in its arguments and also embrace science as a valid source of truth. The discoveries by science in the last fifty years have shed (and will continue to shed) tremendous light on Christian apologetics. If Christianity is to remain a positive force in future generations, Christian theology must absorb scientific discoveries *and* use them to enlighten and give greater insight to faith.

I would be remiss if I didn't mention the encouragement and training I received from two mentors and supervisors I have had on my life journey in both my scientific and theological endeavors. First is the tremendous leadership and training provided by Flight Director and Mission Operations Directorate Director Gene Kranz. Gene was the "straight-arrow" White Flight (flight directors were designated with team colors) who set the example and defined the leadership qualities needed not only for spaceflight operations but also for much of life itself. He taught me the importance of teamwork and good communications skills, to stand up for what I believe, and to realize the importance and timing of correct decision-making.

Second are the wonderful mentoring and pastoral leadership skills I received from my former pastor of some twenty-two years, Judson Edwards. Jud is a wonderful blend of integrity and wisdom and provided me a role model for Christian ministry. His encouragement, leadership style, and articulation of theological truths have given guidance for much of my life, for which I am forever grateful.

Notes

1. John C. Polkinghorne, *Science and Creation* (London: SPCK, 1988) 69.

2. Walt Martin and Magda Ott, eds., *The Cosmic View of Albert Einstein* (New York: Sterling Publishing, 2013) 27.

3. Jeffrey G. Sobosan, *Romancing the Universe* (Grand Rapids MI: Wm. B. Eerdmans, 1999) 4.

Chapter 1

The Race to the Moon

Jump-started by a sound heard around the world.

On October 4, 1957, the world heard something that it had never heard before. To the shock of the United States and the rest of the world, the Russians began the space race with the dramatic launch of a 184-pound basketball-sized Earth satellite called *Sputnik*. It circled the globe every ninety-six minutes and emitted a continuous "beep, beep, beep." The world reacted with shock and fear. Blaring headlines from around the free world repeated that *Sputnik* was circling the Earth with incredible speed. The United States had been considered the world's technological leader, with the Russians lagging far behind. Now, with the launch of the satellite, the Soviets were seen as technologically formidable, having the power to send a rocket with nuclear capability across oceans and into the United States.

At the Redstone Arsenal in Alabama on the evening of the *Sputnik* launch, top brass from Washington were meeting with a team of scientists led by Werner von Braun, who had come to the US after the war. Von Braun and the Army were working on the development of a new Redstone booster rocket but had not had much support from Washington over the past several years. The Eisenhower administration had ignored hints from Moscow that the Soviets were developing the technology to put a satellite in space first. Von Braun knew the Russians were getting close and pleaded with the secretary of defense designate, Neil McElroy, for the go-ahead to speed up development of the Redstone Program. He and his team felt they could get something into orbit within sixty days.[1] However, McElroy said he didn't have the authority to give von Braun the go-ahead at that time.

The United States was soon upstaged again when *Sputnik 2* was launched some thirty days after the first. This time the payload weighed 1,120 pounds and reached an altitude of 1,031 miles. But more astonishing than the increased payload size and altitude, the second satellite carried a dog named Laika. Congress, alarmed by the perceived threat to national security and technological leadership, called for immediate action.[2]

Now under pressure, the Eisenhower administration urged the Vanguard team to get something into orbit. On December 7, two months after *Sputnik* had launched, the US team held its breath as the *Vanguard* rocket fired. It was an embarrassing failure; the *Vanguard* lurched forward and fell backward, breaking apart into a giant fireball. The failure generated feelings of lost confidence and wounded pride in the US program. President Eisenhower gave the Army and von Braun the go-ahead to move forward with von Braun's creation, a modified Redstone rocket (called Jupiter-C), and make it ready to launch a payload. More reliable upper-stage rockets were added, and a thirty-one-pound payload named *Explorer-I* was mounted to the stack. After days of delays caused by high winds, on January 31, 1958, the *Explorer-I* roared into orbit and the US was catapulted into the Space Age.[3] In 1958, President Eisenhower established the National Aeronautics and Space Administration (NASA), though with a distinctly civilian (rather than military) orientation that encouraged peaceful applications in space science.

A number of unmanned flights by the United States and Russia soon followed. Several animals were launched to test the rigors and environment of space flight. The first animal on an American craft was a monkey named Gordo, who survived reentry after a suborbital flight on December 13, 1958, but drowned when the nose cone sank before it could be retrieved. The initial overall NASA strategy to send a man to the Moon and return him safely involved the Mercury Project to test manned orbital capability, followed by the Apollo Program, which would culminate in a lunar landing and a safe return. The objectives of the Mercury Project were to orbit a manned spacecraft around Earth and investigate the basic ability to function in space. The Gemini Program was conceived and added after it became evident that an intermediate step was required between the Mercury Project and the Apollo Program.

On April 9, 1959, NASA announced the Mercury astronauts, who became known as the Mercury 7. The astronauts were first and foremost test pilots, accustomed to flying in the newest, most advanced, and most powerful vehicles technology had produced. They were brave volunteers who would dare to ride the rockets that often exploded into fireballs over Cape Canaveral.

On April 12, 1961, the Russians surged ahead again in the space race with the first man to visit outer space, Yuri Gagarin. Gagarin piloted the *Vostok I* mission on a single orbit of the Earth in a flight lasting 108 minutes. The United States followed on May 5, 1961, with the first astronaut in space, Alan Shepard, whose suborbital flight of the *Freedom 7* space capsule marked the first success of the Mercury Project. On February 20, 1962, the United States finally put a man into orbit when John Glenn piloted *Friendship 7* on three orbits of the Earth. Glenn's success restored some of the self-respect and confidence in the US space program. There followed a succession of three more Mercury flights over the following fifteen months, which culminated with "Gordo" Cooper's flight that went for twenty-two orbits. The Mercury Project spanned some four and a half years and included six manned flights. It accomplished its major objectives, although its final achievement, keeping an astronaut aloft for more than twenty-four hours, had been accomplished by the Soviet Union almost two years earlier.

It was during those formative years of my own life (high school/college) that the mysteries of space flight and electrical systems buzzed around in my head. In 1959, I entered the University of

Texas at Arlington (then Arlington State College), which was close to my home in Fort Worth, Texas. With an aptitude toward math and science, I majored in electrical engineering. As I began to study physics, electron flow, and the vastness of space, there were questions and stirrings in my heart and mind as I marveled at the immensity and grandeur of our universe. The early 1960s was an exciting time in the field of science and engineering, as new knowledge and discoveries were revealed seemingly every day. There were breakthroughs in particle flow, computer technology, and the understanding of our universe. Transistors were breaking into the scene of electrical circuitry. I will never forget the huge equations we dealt with in circuit analysis.

Then, somewhat providentially for my sake, on May 25, 1961, before a joint session of Congress, President John F. Kennedy challenged the nation with the goal of "landing a man on the moon and returning him safely to the Earth by the end of the decade." Then, on September 12, 1962, at Rice University in Houston, President Kennedy again echoed this challenge to go to the Moon with the famous words, "We choose to go to the moon, and do other things, not because they are easy, but because they are hard."[4] The inspiring words resonated with me and gave new energy and motivation to the space program. I felt I wanted to be a part of that program. People often ask even today, why go to the Moon? Why go to Mars? Why invest such large sums of money and time and energy when those resources could be used more productively down here on Earth? Of course, in the 1960s the decision to go to the Moon was primarily based on political and military reasons. The United States was locked in a cold war with the Soviet Union, and whoever could launch an orbital rocket or maintain a Moon base stood to gain a tremendous advantage.

However, I think the rationale and drive to go to the Moon or embark on any kind of interplanetary space travel goes much deeper and is more basic than a military motivation. It is a search for truth. Humanity has been enamored by travel to the Moon and Mars for a hundred years or more. Like explorers of the fifteenth and sixteenth centuries who sought truths and new discoveries in foreign lands, modern-day space explorers look for new discoveries and answers to fundamental life questions: What will investigations on a foreign body tell us about life? What can the planets tell us about the history and structure of the universe? Is there life on other planets? As Einstein would ask, do we live in a cold and hostile universe? In a deeper sense, as John Polkinghorne would ask, is there purpose behind the 14-billion-year-old sweep of cosmic history, or do we live in a world devoid of ultimate meaning?[5] Space travelers can help us find the answers to these questions, and I was excited to throw my lot into the mix with these travelers.

My involvement with NASA began as soon as I graduated from the University of Texas at Arlington in 1964. I was fortunate to join NASA that year, as they had just begun the manned phase of the Gemini Program. Reflecting back, I can see what I believe was a guiding hand from above that allowed me to join the NASA team in Houston. Graduating with an engineering degree in the early sixties was an open door for meaningful employment, as my fellow graduates were getting multiple offers from Texas Instruments, North American Rockwell, IBM, General Dynamics, and other big-name organizations. Down deep, I secretly had a dream to work at NASA; but like any responsible graduate I sent my application to all the above organizations. Even though I had good grades, I received only one offer. If I wanted to eat, I needed to move to Houston and join the NASA team. I was thrilled.

At NASA I was assigned to the Mission Operations Directorate as a systems engineer in the Flight Operations Division. It was an exciting period in the development of the Johnson Space Center (then called the Manned Spacecraft Center), as I had arrived at an opportune time for the buildup of the new center in Houston and the beginning of the manned phase of the Gemini Program. Our team had the task of designing the structure and operation of the new Mission Operation Control Room (MOCR), which was under construction. The more pressing task, however, was learning the systems operations, developing procedures, and testing the new systems on the *Gemini* spacecraft. Multiple trips to the McDonnell Aircraft plant in St. Louis to test systems operations of the *Gemini* spacecraft were involved. Strategically, *Gemini* was the bridge between *Mercury* and *Apollo*. It would not only test the space worthiness of many new spacecraft systems but would also provide experience and demonstrate the capability to rendezvous and dock with another vehicle in space, which was an essential building block in the critical *Apollo* Moon landing recovery scenario. Also, where *Mercury* was a single manned capsule above a Redstone or Atlas booster, *Gemini* was a two-manned vehicle mated with the powerful Titan booster.

In those early days of flight operations, even though the crew operated and "flew" the vehicle in some respects, the ground controllers (or flight controllers, as we were called) provided systems monitoring to hundreds of parameters (pressures, temperatures, voltages, currents, control system gimbal angles, etc.), which were downlinked from the vehicle and served to aid us in diagnosing problems, selecting alternate systems, performing routine system management, and making go/no-go decisions at critical flight junctures. It was an exciting and challenging time, as new systems were subjected to rigorous testing here on Earth, and then faced the harshness of outer space for the first time. I was assigned as junior engineer in the Gemini electrical, environmental, and communications systems section. Many systems—fuel cells, mini-computers, engines, and environmental control systems—were new to the manned *Gemini* vehicle. As flight operations engineers, we had two types of jobs. Our office job included developing flight procedures, mission rules, and operational engineering drawings, as well as designing the monitoring devices for the missions. Additionally, our mission support involved not only console operations during the flight but also hours and hours of training and simulations in a flight-type environment.

The first two *Gemini* flights (*I* and *II*) were unmanned and used to qualify the new *Gemini* Titan II rocket combination. The third mission, *Gemini III*, was the first manned flight and was flown by Gus Grissom and John Young in March 1965. For *Gemini III*, Mission Control was centered at the Cape while the Mission Control Complex in Houston was being completed. *Gemini III* was to be a three-orbit mission involving a number of maneuvers to check the propulsion and guidance systems and the new onboard computer, the

THE RACE TO THE MOON

first ever used in space. The *Gemini III* spacecraft was dubbed *Molly Brown* (after the "unsinkable" heroine of the Broadway musical) by astronauts Grissom and Young after Grissom's first spacecraft, *Liberty Bell 7*, sank.

For early flights, prior to routing all the data to Houston, mission operations were carried out with support of a flight control team deployed to remote sites that were strategically located along the ground track around the globe. The team consisted of engineers, technicians, a medical doctor, and a capsule communicator (Cap Com). I was lucky to be assigned as a junior Gemini systems engineer at the Carnarvon, Australia, site for this first manned flight. Carnarvon was important because it was one of the critical sites in preparation for the deorbit and landing phase of the mission.

As with most of these flights, there were always interesting stories that accompanied the remote site trips. One such story for this flight is that our team of engineers and technicians was deployed to Australia several weeks early to get the site ready for the mission. However, the Cap Com, in this case Pete Conrad, came later, on a separate flight just five days prior to launch. As it turns out, there was a major flap between Conrad and Dan Hunter (our local operations director) on who should be in charge. The astronauts felt they should be in charge and the only ones communicating with the crew during the mission. The flap escalated to the level of Christopher Kraft (missions ops director) and Deke Slayton (crew operations chief), and Kraft gave Hunter the role of site operations director while Conrad was to be in charge during flight operations. (Because of this incident, after the flight, Kraft cut a deal with Slayton that gave the crew communications control of the spacecraft and gave the ground team command of the mission.)[6]

Another funny part of the incident was that the Carnarvon site was in the middle of nowhere on the Australian west coast, and our quarters were like military dorm rooms. We all ate together at a hotel-like dining hall, and in those days most of the young engineers dressed alike, with crew-cut hair that typically resembled an astronaut's cut. The strange thing was that, prior to Conrad arriving, for every meal I was always given a double portion of food and special room service morning and evening. The staff asked for my autograph, and I was treated royally. The special treatment came to an abrupt end when Conrad arrived. To my surprise, I learned that the hotel staff had thought I was the astronaut. No more supersized desserts or special room service for me!

The *Gemini III* mission was considered a major success despite a few thruster issues and the sudden appearance of a contraband corned beef sandwich. The flight success was an exciting moment in US space program history, for it proved that the US could do just as well as the Soviets and that the US now had a fighting chance in the space race.

Building on the success of *Gemini III, Gemini IV* was launched in June 1965 with Jim McDivitt and Ed White selected as the flight crew. The Houston Mission Control Center became operational, and I was assigned as a system engineer in one of the staff support rooms. This was the most ambitious flight to date. It would not only stay in orbit four days but would also have the astronauts attempt America's first spacewalk. Ed White became the first American to venture outside his spacecraft for what is officially known as an "extravehicular activity," or EVA. The world has come to know it as a "spacewalk." In the following years, it was a skill that allowed Apollo explorers to walk on the Moon. On the ground, our team now monitored the vehicle's systems health as well as the parameters associated with the space suit and its support system.

The next mission, *Gemini V*, set a space endurance record. Gordon Cooper and Pete Conrad spent almost eight days in space, traveling 3.3 million miles in orbits around the Earth. The spacecraft experienced several technical issues during the flight, however, including problems with our fuel cell that put off a planned rendezvous experiment. Oxygen pressure on the fuel cell dropped from 850 pounds per square inch absolute (psia) to around 85 psia. The crew determined that the heater in the oxygen system had failed to operate. The spacecraft was powered down, and the rendezvous test was abandoned. We knew the spacecraft had enough battery power for reentry even if the fuel cell failed completely, but we had to determine if there would be enough time to reach a good reentry zone,

THE RACE TO THE MOON   13

such as the mid-Pacific near Hawaii, on the sixth revolution. It was our first major problem at the new Mission Control Center (MCC), and it happened to be on a system our team was responsible for.

One of our support engineers at the McDonnell facility in St. Louis was a strong Christian, and for the first time he and I prayed that the Lord would somehow restore this mechanical system. What's wrong with praying for mechanical systems? The Good Book says to pray for everything! Engineers at McDonnell quickly arranged tests to find out the lowest working pressure for a fuel cell. During the fourth revolution, the oxygen pressure gradually stabilized at around 70 psia, and then, miraculously, it increased through the remainder of the mission. By the seventh revolution, based on results from our support in St. Louis, we had determined that the fuel cells could work even at lower pressures.

With this reassurance, our team and Flight Director Gene Kranz decided to tell Cooper and Conrad to turn the electricity back on. We were relieved when the fuel cells were restarted and tested using equipment that required more and more power. This showed that the fuel cell pressure had stabilized, and the crew could continue its mission. The *Gemini V* crew went on to work on other experiments planned for the mission, including an alternative rendezvous test worked out by fellow astronaut Buzz Aldrin on the ground. After all the problems, the crew returned to Earth following some eight days in space. *Gemini V* marked a milestone in the space race, as the accumulated time in space put the Americans ahead of the Soviets for that marker.

With the basics of multiday space flight down, our next task to be performed was a rendezvous of two vehicles in space. The Russians had tried twice and failed, but we were impressed by their dual launch capability. The plan was to launch an Agena target vehicle on a separate launch pad and then launch *Gemini VI* with Wally Schirra and Tom Stafford to chase down and rendezvous. However, to our dismay, the Agena exploded during the launch phase, and the plan was foiled. The agency then decided to combine the activities of Schirra and Stafford with the upcoming *Gemini VII* two-week endurance mission. Frank Borman and Jim Lovell blasted off on

December 4, 1965, with the newly named *Gemini VIa* to follow. On the *Gemini VIa* planned launch day of December 12, however, the Titan II rocket shut down only two seconds after its ignition. Schirra elected not to eject, and another launch was attempted three days later without major incident. As planned, the two spacecrafts then made a close approach in space.

Even though rendezvous capability had been demonstrated with *Geminis VI* and *VII*, the ability to link two spaceships in orbit still had to be proven. That task was assigned to the *Gemini VIII* crew, Neil Armstrong and Dave Scott, who would dock with the Agena target vehicle launched separately by an Atlas rocket. *Gemini VIII* launched March 16, 1966, and successfully docked with the Agena target vehicle a little over six hours after liftoff. Not long after the docking, however, the combined *Gemini*/target vehicle began experiencing increasing roll and yaw rates. The crew undocked with the Agena, but our Cap Com at the Coastal Century remote site reported roll rates up to 360 degrees per second. There was something wrong with the Gemini control system. All we could do at the MCC was pray. On the verge of losing consciousness from the accelerating spin, the crew finally regained control of their spacecraft by using the reentry control system, which prompted an early landing at a secondary landing site in the Pacific. No EVA was performed. The failure was caused by an electrical short in the control system. The crew returned safely, but we thanked the Good Lord again and the exceptional efforts of the crew, who made a fantastic recovery under such circumstances.

The last few Gemini missions were mostly devoted to figuring out advanced docking techniques as well as nailing down how to perform a spacewalk. In the earlier missions, astronauts found themselves struggling and exhausted as they tried to cling to the side of a spacecraft in zero gravity. Learning from our experience, EVA engineers added additional handholds and footholds to make the EVA easier.

For me, the Gemini flights were a tremendous learning experience of flight control discipline and vehicle operations while managing problematic systems. We had established the basics of manned spacecraft operations and demonstrated vehicle rendezvous capability. Little did we know the challenges that lay ahead. It's often quite interesting how many times God prepares us with challenges in one area for even greater challenges in the future.

Notes

1. Alan Shepard and Deke Slayton, *Moon Shot* (Atlanta: Turner Publishing, Inc., 1994) 40.

2. Ibid., 44.

3. Ibid., 45, 48.

4. "We choose to go to the Moon," Wikipedia last updated 11 April 2016, https://en.wikipedia.org/wiki/We_choose_to_go_to_the_Moon.

5. John C. Polkinghorne, *Science and Creation* (London: SPCK, 1988) 1f.

6. Eugene F. Kranz, *Failure Is Not an Option* (New York: Simon & Schuster, 2000) 131.

Chapter 2

Apollo–Landing on the Moon

"That's one small step for [a] man, one giant leap for mankind."

With the basic mechanics of spaceflight now behind us, NASA now embarked on the final program to reach the Moon—Apollo. It was an ambitious program with new vehicles, new systems, new engines, and a new booster rocket, the mighty Saturn V. It's helpful at this point to describe the overall vehicle stack. The complete assembly, including the *Apollo* spacecraft and the Saturn launch vehicle, stood 363 feet tall and weighed more than 6 million pounds. The Saturn V launch vehicle itself consisted of three stages: (1) The first stage (S-I C) included the five Saturn engines producing nearly 7.7 million pounds of thrust. These powerful engines were required to lift the heavy rocket fast enough to escape Earth's gravity. The first stage then separated and burned up in the Earth's atmosphere. (2) The second stage (S-II) contained five J-2 engines and burned for approximately 6 minutes, taking the vehicle and payload to 115 miles altitude. The second stage was then also discarded. (3) The third stage (S-IV B) contained one J-2 engine and burned for about 3 minutes, boosting the spacecraft to orbital velocity. The third stage was shut down with fuel remaining and stayed attached to the spacecraft in Earth orbit.

The S-IV B was reignited to propel the spacecraft into translunar trajectory before finally being discarded.

Above the booster stages was the payload vehicle, or, on our lunar flights, the Command and Service Module (CSM) and the Lunar Module (LM). The CSM consisted of two sections: the Command Module (CM), which was the crew compartment and housed three astronauts and all the displays and controls; and the Service Module, which was essentially an engine room, housing the fuel, the electrical system, the oxygen, and the main engine that was required to enter and leave lunar orbit. The LM was a spiderlike vehicle with an ascent and descent stage that two astronauts would board for landing on the Moon. The LM was unique. It was the first vehicle to operate exclusively in the vacuum of space, and as such, it had no heat shield or aerodynamic lines for it to withstand reentry heating. Its external skin was paper-thin aluminum. You could kick your boot through it if not careful. The lower stage or descent stage housed the propulsion systems and propellant to get the craft down to the Moon's surface. Four tall rather spindly legs with four giant foot pads were attached. The ascent stage contained the living quarters, controls, displays, guidance and navigation, and ascent engine used for launch from the Moon's surface and maneuvers. It also housed the batteries, environmental control system, communications, and a state-of-the-art computer with a 36.8K fixed memory. During launch the LM was covered by a cone-like adapter shroud. After reaching orbit, the four sections of the adapter were jettisoned. The CSM then turned around, docked with the LM, and extracted it from the booster.

After the last Gemini flight (*Gemini XII*), I was assigned to the LM Systems Branch under Jim Hannigan. The LM systems responsibility was broken down into two major disciplines: (1) the propulsion, guidance, and navigation systems, and (2) the telemetry, electrical power, life support, and communications systems (or TELCOM). I was fortunate to be assigned to the TELCOM Section under Don Puddy, which of course was my favorite area due to my engineering background. We focused on development of operational systems drawings, procedures, and mission rules for the upcoming flights. In 1966 there were several unmanned tests of the Apollo Saturn to test

APOLLO—LANDING ON THE MOON

the space worthiness of the Saturn and vehicle capability. Our LM crew of engineers made several trips to the Grumman Engineering plant in Bethpage, New York, to gather data and observe testing of the LM.

On January 27, 1967, tragedy hit the US space program like a sledgehammer. The *Apollo 1* spacecraft with Gus Grissom, Ed White, and Roger Chaffee was undergoing a full up pad test at the Cape. I was not assigned to the test since the Lunar Module was not involved. At around 5:31 p.m. that fateful Friday evening, a brief voice report from the crew in the cockpit jolted the launch and flight teams: "We've got fire in the cockpit." There was a gallant but futile attempt to rescue the crew, but the hatch could not be opened. All three lives were snuffed out in a raging inferno within the *Apollo 1* capsule. It was never really concluded what initiated the spark, but unfortunately the cabin was pressurized with pure oxygen, and there were many combustible materials within it. Death had come to the space program in a most unimaginable way—to three helpless men who were not even in space but in a cockpit just 318 feet above the ground.[1] The astronauts and the flight team always knew there were risks to space flight, but this drove home the point to NASA and the American public of the risks in exploring the heavens.

The accident profoundly affected everyone at NASA. Our leader in Flight Operations, Gene Kranz, whom I looked up to the most, was dreadfully shaken but resolved to move forward. A review board was appointed to investigate the accident. That next week Gene called a meeting of the controllers at which he said,

> From this day forward, Flight Control will be known by two words: "Tough and Competent." *Tough* means we are forever accountable for what we do or what we fail to do. We will never again compromise our responsibilities. *Competent* means we will never take anything for granted. We will never be found short in our knowledge and in our skills.[2]

I was shaken as well, and from that day forward I resolved always to give my best effort for whatever task I was called to do. In my own soul, of course, I wondered—like with any tragedy—why something like this would happen. I couldn't come up with any real answers except to believe that God had created a world that operated, for the most part, under certain physical laws, and that in this case he chose not to suspend those laws.

In the aftermath of the accident, changes were made to the vehicle and operating procedures (for example, the breathable atmosphere was changed to be composed of an oxygen/nitrogen mixture much like our own atmosphere; the hatch was redesigned to make it more operable from the inside; and several fire-retardant materials were developed for such items as the crew suits). By the fall of 1967, the program emerged from the crisis, and testing on the rebuilt Apollo resumed. *Apollo 4*, *5*, and *6* were unmanned tests of the Saturn launch vehicle and the Lunar Module as well. There was no *Apollo 2* or *3*. Successful testing paved the way for a return to manned flight with *Apollo 7*. *Apollo 7* launched on October 11, 1968, and was crewed by Wally Schirra, Donn Eisele, and Walt Cunningham. The launch went smoothly, with the Saturn rocket blasting the CSM into Earth orbit. It was an eleven-day Earth-orbital flight that tested the CSM systems.

Apollo 8 was originally planned to be an Earth-orbit manned test of the CSM and the LM to be launched in December 1968. In the summer it became clear that the LM would not be ready in time for that mission. The LM was overweight, and the software development was running behind. Rather than waste the Saturn V on another simple Earth-orbiting mission, NASA managers suggested the bold step of sending *Apollo 8* to orbit the Moon instead, without the lunar lander and eliminating a high Earth-orbit mission. This would keep the program on track. The Soviet Union had sent animals around the Moon on September 15, 1968, and it was believed they might soon repeat the feat with human cosmonauts. The decision to orbit the Moon was not announced publicly until successful completion of *Apollo 7*.

Apollo 8 was launched on December 21, 1968, and was the first manned mission to go to the Moon. Although I was not assigned to the flight, since it had no LM or lunar landing, it was an exciting mission, as astronauts Frank Borman, James Lovell, and William

Anders were the first humans to pull away from Earth orbit and go into translunar coast. They were the first to capture that famous picture of planet Earth as it appears like a beautiful blue marble dangling in space. Looking at the Earth from that perspective, you realize how uniquely different and small we are. *Apollo 8* successfully went into lunar orbit and made ten orbits around the Moon, while transmitting some outstanding television pictures of the lunar surface to the Earth.

Then, on Christmas Eve 1968, while millions of people brought their families together, Bill Anders spoke on the downlink, not just to the NASA team, but to the whole world listening below. "For all the people on Earth," he said, "the crew of *Apollo 8* has a message we would like to send you." After a brief pause, Anders stunned his audience as he began reading from the book of Genesis:

> In the beginning, God created the heaven and the earth. Now the earth was without form and empty, darkness was over the surface of the deep, and the Spirit of God was hovering over the waters. And God said, "Let there be light," and there was light. God saw that the light was good, and he separated the light from the darkness.

As he concluded verse 4, Lovell then read the next four verses, and Borman ended with his reading of the ninth verse. Then he sent a special Christmas message: "And from the crew of *Apollo 8*, we close with good night, good luck, a Merry Christmas, and may God bless all of you—all of you on the good Earth." My heart was stirred, as I'm sure thousands more were, as we realized how uniquely small we are in the universe. And here from ancient times, a word from somewhere in space declared a sort of dual message: that there is a beginning to our universe and there is a God who can bless us. For John Aaron, the CSM Electrical, Environmental, and Consumables Manager (EECOM), and many more in the control room that day, the Genesis reading was a perfect capstone for what had been to that point a perfect flight. Aaron later reflected, "It was the most overwhelming thing that has ever happened to me in my life, just because it was not only a surprise, it was *so* appropriate."[3] For me there was the realization that this God of the universe had visited us, on this very anniversary night some 2,000 years ago, as a Child at Christmas.

The following March of 1969, *Apollo 9* was launched, piloted by James McDivitt, Dave Scott, and Rusty Schweickart. It was primarily the LM check-out flight, although it was done in Earth orbit only. The LM was activated and the descent engine fired with the vehicles attached. A rendezvous and docking were successfully demonstrated in Earth orbit. This was a great thrill for our LM flight control team as, for the first time, we got to see LM data from orbit. On the fourth day, the LM was depressurized and the LM pilot (Schweickart) exited the LM hatch for an EVA wearing the Extravehicular Mobility Unit (EMU), which provided the oxygen, cooling, and communications needed to survive in space. The mission flew successfully and proved the LM worthy of manned spaceflight.

After *Apollo 9*, I was promoted to what was called the Missions Operations Control Room in the MCC. Moving to the front room was a dream come true, for it was where the flights were controlled. During this phase of the space program—in my opinion—there was no greater place for a scientist or engineer to work. In the sixties and seventies, we felt we were on the cutting edge of scientific advancement, and the Missions Operations Control Room represented the heart and soul of the scientific world.

The responsibility of control and monitoring of the flight was divided up among eight to ten major engineering positions that worked in the Mission Operations Control Room, and each was supported by another crew of support personnel in back rooms. Each position had a call sign or name, and my position was called TELCOM, which was an acronym that stood for Telemetry, Electrical Power, Life Support, and the Communications systems of the Lunar Module.

Apollo 10 was successfully launched on May 18, 1969, and crewed by Gemini veterans Thomas Stafford, John Young, and Eugene Cernan. All the components of *Apollo 10* were similar to those for *Apollo 9*, the major difference being the inclusion of a fully configured LM. *Apollo 10* was a "dress rehearsal" for the landing missions that would follow, and as such it was a fully configured spacecraft.

Stafford and Cernan separated the LM from the CSM and took the LM down to within 50,000 feet of the lunar surface; however, this LM was an early design that could not be used for a landing, as it was too heavy to return to orbit from the lunar surface.

July 16, 1969, the day of the launch of our *Apollo 11* lunar landing mission, had finally arrived. It was, of course, the culmination of what had been planned in detail for the last five years and the reality of what President Kennedy had challenged our nation to some eight years earlier. We had undergone hours and hours of simulation and training, facing every imaginal malicious scenario that our training team could think of. The crew, Neil Armstrong, Buzz Aldrin, and Mike Collins, had undergone numerous hours of training as well. Neil had been selected to be the commander of this famous flight, probably because of his excellent piloting skills demonstrated under pressure with *Gemini VIII*. The adrenaline was flowing in our LM team as well, even though we wouldn't get to see LM data until the fourth day of the flight. Due to the electrical power margin, the LM would not be powered up and checked out until shortly before lunar landing. I was assigned to the Black Team under Flight Director Glynn Lunney. We had four teams of flight controllers that were necessary for the various phases of the mission. Don Puddy, our lead TELCOM, had the lunar landing shift under Flight Director Gene Kranz. Our team had the post-liftoff phase.

Apollo 11 successfully launched on July 16, 1969, and about one and a half revolutions later the S-IV B booster stage ignited and placed *Apollo 11* into translunar orbit. The CSM, nicknamed *Columbia*, separated from the booster stage, and after the jettisoning of the LM shroud adapter panels, it separated from the LM and booster. It then made the transposition maneuver, docked, and extracted the LM from the booster stage—and we were on our way. The LM was nicknamed *Eagle*. The first color TV transmission to Earth from *Apollo 11* occurred during the translunar coast. Later, on July 17, a three-second burn of the CSM engine was made to perform one of the scheduled midcourse corrections programmed for the flight. All went well. The launch had been so successful that the other three burns were not needed.

On July 18, Armstrong and Aldrin put on their spacesuits and climbed through the docking tunnel from *Columbia* to *Eagle* to check out the LM and make a TV transmission. Although we didn't get to see any LM data, at least from the TV viewing our spacecraft seemed to have arrived in space without any trouble. Our only clue to the health of the LM was a CSM heater current (amperage) that was passed to the LM to keep critical components warm.

On landing day, July 20, the Mission Control Center was buzzing with excitement. A small army of flight controllers was riveted to their consoles with every eye intently watching their data. The CSM/LM was now in orbit around the Moon, and Neil and Buzz entered the LM and began its check-out. The landing gear was deployed and the large steerable antenna powered up. For the first time, we could see a complete set of LM telemetry data. Puddy's team quickly assessed our LM data and gave a happy "Go" to the flight director. Shortly afterward, White Flight (Kranz) polled the whole control room for a "Go/No Go" for undocking. A number of "Go/No Go" points had been identified at critical junctures in the flight plan. The poll was made quickly, with all controllers giving a "Go" for undocking, and Charlie Duke, our landing team Cap Com, passed the "Go" along to the crew. The emotion in the control room was mixed with tension and excitement as the LM separated from the CSM and began its descent to the lunar surface.

As the LM made its journey on the far side of the Moon, Gene Kranz asked that all controllers switch over to a private AFD (Assistant Flight Director) communication loop where only the control room could hear. Gene spoke from a heart filled with emotion:

> Today is our day, and the hopes and dreams of the entire world are with us. This is our time and our place, and we will remember this day and what we will do here always. In the next hour we will do something that has never been done before. We will land an American on the moon. The risks are high . . . that is the nature of our work. . . . You are a hell of a good team. One I feel privileged to lead. Whatever happens, I stand behind every call that you make. Good luck, and God bless us today.[4]

As a team, we felt molded together, on the brink of history, ready to step out with Neil and Buzz where no other human had ever walked before.

Even though not officially assigned to this phase of the mission, all our primary team personnel were in the Mission Operations Control Room for this exciting event, and we sat on a small ledge behind various consoles where we could follow the landing events. The emotion in the room was at a peak as the flight control team gave a "Go" for landing, despite intermittent data and communications problems. The final landing phase itself was only about twelve minutes, but the mood was electric. As the *Eagle* made its descent to the Moon, a critical computer program alarm went off both onboard and on the ground. It was assessed by Steve Bales, the guidance engineer, but given a "Go" for landing. All flight controllers were "Go." Bob Carlton, our LM control engineer, called out fuel remaining in the LM as the crew called out altitude and descent rate. The crew called "3,000 feet" as Neil maneuvered the bug-like spacecraft over huge boulders, rocks, and deadly craters. A second computer alarm sounded. Bales advised again, "Same type . . . we're 'Go.'" The crew and Carlton continued their call-outs as all eyes were glued to their data. As the crew passed seventy-five feet, Carlton sounded, "Sixty seconds." The LM needed to land within sixty seconds or the fuel would be depleted. The crew called out, "Forty feet, picking up dust, thirty feet, seeing a shadow." Then the crew called, "Contact . . . engine stop." The vehicle had landed. Charlie Duke responded, "We copy you down, *Eagle*." Then, while the anxious world waited, Neil called down, "Houston, Tranquility Base here. The *Eagle* has landed." Charlie Duke responded, "Roger, Tranquility. We copy you on the ground. You got a bunch of guys here about to turn blue. We're breathing again. Thanks a lot."[5]

A feeling of euphoria swept over the room as a team full of controllers were cheering and clapping. Charlie Duke opened his microphone, and the celebration inside the MOCR echoed across a quarter-million miles and brought a smile to Neil and Buzz. Without a break, White Flight quickly polled the team again for a "Stay" or

"No Stay" for lunar surface operations. All systems looked good, and the "Stay" was given.

Then, shortly after touchdown in the cramped quarters of the LM cockpit, something happened that was never published at the time. Buzz Aldrin celebrated the first and only Lord's Supper on the Moon. Inside the LM, just hours before stepping onto the lunar surface for the first time, Aldrin radioed Mission Control. He asked for a few moments of silence "to invite each person listening, wherever and whomever they may be, to pause for a moment and contemplate the events of the past few hours, and to give thanks in his or her own way." In the moment of silence that followed, Aldrin read a passage in the Bible that he had personally written out from the Gospel of John: "I am the vine, you are the branches. Whoever remains in me, and I in him, will bear much fruit; for you can do nothing without me." Then he took out a miniature chalice and bread and wine from his personal allowance pouch. "I poured the wine into the chalice our church had given me," he told *Guideposts* magazine in 1970. "In the one-sixth gravity of the moon, the wine curled slowly and gracefully up the side of the cup. It was interesting to think that the very first liquid ever poured on the moon, and the first food eaten there, were communion elements."[6] Even though I wasn't aware of it at the time, I now reflect some forty-eight years later and marvel at the design of the universe, the laws that control it, and how God allows humanity to participate with those laws in the search for truth. But I also realize how the very bread and wine eaten and drunk by Buzz on this first lunar landing represented the body and blood of the incarnate Christ, given so that we on planet Earth might know truth.

About five hours after landing, the crew suited up for the first walk on the Moon's surface. The LM cabin was depressurized, and Neil Armstrong climbed down the ladder and became the first human to step out onto the lunar surface. As millions watched on TV, he spoke into his spacesuit radio and uttered those now famous words: "That's one small step for man, and one giant leap for mankind." Americans had made it to the Moon. The US had met the challenge.

A few minutes later, Buzz climbed down the ladder, and the crew bounded across the lunar landscape like kangaroos. Our TELCOM team continued to monitor the health and status of the LM systems, and the EMU team monitored the crew's suit pressures and temperatures as they were downlinked on telemetry.

Rocks and boulders littered the lunar landscape. Neil and Buzz were both awed by the stark desolation of the Moon's surface. Neil voiced on his radio, "It has a very stark beauty of its own." Buzz commented, "Beautiful, magnificent desolation." As we continued to watch in amazement, they jammed a pole into the lunar subsoil with the US flag attached. Then, standing back from the *Eagle*, they saw something no other human had ever seen before: a beautiful Earth shimmering over the lunar horizon. The Moon stood in stark gray contrast—no clouds, no atmosphere, no oceans, no green grass, no birds . . . no life.

The crew gathered some fifty pounds of lunar soil samples and returned to the cabin after about two and a half hours of EVA. After LM repressurization and removal of their EMUs, they tried to sleep as best they could. Then, some twenty-one hours after touchdown, the crew fired up the *Eagle* ascent engine and blasted off from the lunar surface, leaving the descent stage behind. The crew skillfully flew the *Eagle* back to rendezvous with *Columbia*, where Michael Collins was eagerly awaiting. After docking and after the crew transferred back into the CSM, the faithful *Eagle* was undocked and left in lunar orbit to eventually decay into the Moon. It had been a spaceworthy vehicle, one that we were proud to design and operate. The return trip home took about three days, and the Command Module landed safely in the Pacific.

After *Apollo 11*, the lunar program was focused on pinpoint landings and extending the duration and complexity of the lunar excursions. *Apollo 12* was targeted to land near *Surveyor 3*, an unmanned spacecraft that had landed just three years earlier. *Surveyor 3* was resting in a 700-foot-wide crater in the Moon's "Ocean of Storms." The crew for *Apollo 12* was an all-Navy crew—Pete Conrad, whom I got to know from my Carnarvon experience; Dick Gordon; and Al Bean. Conrad and Bean were the LM pilots, and the landing required a high degree of precision.

Gerry Griffin, the Gold Team Flight Director, was on duty for the launch, and for this flight I was assigned to the Gold Team. For *Apollo 12* and subsequent missions, there had also been a realignment of some of our systems responsibilities, where all the communications systems were merged into one position called INCO (Instrumentation Communications). Our TELCOM position absorbed the EMU systems responsibility, and we were renamed TELMU (where MU reflected responsibility for the Extravehicular Mobility Unit).

It had been raining on November 14, the morning of the *Apollo 12* launch. As the launch proceeded, the Saturn soon disappeared into the overcast sky. Conrad reported, "This baby is really moving." Gordon called out, "Looking good," but then followed shortly by "Uh-oh!" On board, the amber lights of the caution and warning panels flashed on. The ground displays experienced multiple data dropouts. (Unknown to the crew or ground control team, the vehicle had been hit by lightning.) Launch observers on the ground had seen a brilliant flash in the vicinity of the launch complex. Conrad said with amazing calm, "We've got a bunch of alarms. We've just lost our platform." (The platform was a set of gyros that provided the reference for the navigation system.) Fuel cells and main electrical busses were offline. The backup batteries had taken over, and John Aaron, our launch EECOM, prayed that whatever had happened had not shut off the oxygen and hydrogen flow to the fuel cells. If the fuel cell valves had closed, the lunar mission was over unless the fuel cell flow could be restored shortly. Less than a minute into the launch, Flight Director Gerry Griffin knew that the possibility of aborting was strong.[7]

John Aaron was pouring over the data with backroom support. He suddenly remembered an instrumentation situation from a test the year before that was similar to the one they were currently seeing. Precious seconds passed. Griffin called out, "How's it looking, EECOM?" Aaron's next call made him a legend in Mission Control. Without hesitation, he made the decisive call: "Flight, have the crew take the SCE to Aux." (The SCE was the acronym for a Signal Conditioning Equipment power supply used to power critical instrumentation points; Aux meant auxiliary or the alternate power supply.)

Griffin was not aware of the little-known switch. He queried Aaron again, and Aaron repeated himself. Griffin had worked with Aaron intensively and learned to trust him. He passed the command to Cap Com Gerry Carr; the Cap Com made the call to the crew: "Try SCE to Auxiliary, over." Conrad was a bit perplexed like Griffin, but Carr repeated the instruction again. Al Bean reached forward and toggled the switch down. A few moments later Aaron announced, "We've got valid data. Looking good." In less than sixty seconds, the fuel cells were back online and Griffin had a "Go" from all the controllers for orbit.

It was impossible to check out the entire spacecraft, but after running some checks and realigning the platform, the crew was given a "Go" for translunar injection. Conrad and Bean went on to make a pinpoint landing next to the *Surveyor*, establishing a new space record and increasing the duration of lunar surface activity.[8] This had been one of the most challenging launches of any flight in the program, and we thanked the Lord for his watchcare and the quick minds that had the courage to respond in critical situations.

Notes

1. Eugene F. Kranz, *Failure Is Not an Option* (New York: Simon & Schuster, 2000) 199.

2. Ibid., 204.

3. Rick Houston and Milt Heflin, *Go Flight! The Unsung Heroes of Mission Control, 1965-1992* (Lincoln: University of Nebraska Press, 2015) 131.

4. Kranz, *Failure Is Not an Option*, 283.

5. Ibid. 292.

6. Buzz Aldrin, "Communion in Space," *Guideposts,* October 1970 (https://www.guideposts.org/better-living/life-advice/finding-life-purpose/guideposts-classics-buzz-aldrin-on-communion-in-space).

7. Kranz, *Failure Is Not an Option*, 300.

8. Ibid. 303.

Chapter 3

Apollo 13–
The Rest of the Story

"Houston, we've had a problem."

Apollo 13 lifted off on April 11, 1970, under the power of the mighty Saturn V rockets. It was to be our third landing flight to the Moon and more ambitious than our first two. The crew for *Apollo 13* comprised Commander Jim Lovell, Lunar Module pilot Fred Haise, and Command Module pilot Jack Swigert, who had replaced pilot Ken Mattingly just a few weeks prior to launch. The flight plan of *Apollo 13* would have the CSM/LM separate from the booster, leave on translunar trajectory to the Moon, and land at the Fra Mauro site. It was more than 200,000 miles away and would take about three and a half days. For *Apollo 13*, however, there was no lunar landing, no momentous words spoken from the lunar surface, no rocks returned to the Earth.[1]

    Apollo 13 was in one sense a tragic disaster but in another sense a hinge on which my life has turned. For me, the flight of *Apollo 13* was not a failure but a flight of miracles. It was a flight protected by the Creator of life itself, who reached out in a miraculous way to provide a lifeboat for three astronauts whose lives literally hung in the balance of space. It was a miracle not unlike the one God performed for Noah and his family as recorded in the Bible, providing a safe environment for the crew and stretching life-supporting consumables as

Jesus himself had miraculously stretched five loaves of bread and two fish to feed five thousand in the first century. Of course, you may question the possibility of miracles; I will take up that issue in a later chapter.

Why an omnipotent God rescues some (such as the *Apollo 13* crew) and not others (such as the *Apollo 1* crew) is a profound and provocative question. Humans make mistakes and natural processes are allowed to proceed. We may not always know or understand God's ways, but I have come to believe we can trust his heart.

The miraculous recovery of the *Apollo 13* crew was also perhaps the finest example of teamwork in NASA's history. John Aaron, CSM EECOM, has said, "It was almost as if the whole reason we were there culminated in that one moment. The ground controllers worked so well as a team, as we were able to successfully salvage the mission and get the crew home safely."[2] Of course, the disaster and triumph of *Apollo 13* was of such drama and importance that it has been written up several times and made into a full feature-length movie played over and over on many occasions. The movie, I think, was well done and accurately chronicled, although, as one might expect, there were certain Hollywood twists and additions. What the movie doesn't tell you, however, is that there were several miracles, I believe, that came into play, allowing the crew to return safely to Earth. Much like the fuel cell pressure that mysteriously increased on *Gemini V* a few years earlier, I feel that God's hand was hovering over the *Apollo 13* spacecraft, protecting its precious cargo.

At the time, I was a young engineer and fully entrenched at the TELMU position on the Black Team. There were actually four teams that worked various shifts in the Mission Operations Control Room. The Black Team was headed by Flight Director Glynn Lunney, a sharp and perceptive engineer who came out of the flight dynamics ranks and provided a calming leadership to our team. That background became important in our return planning options for *Apollo 13* after the aborted lunar landing and in light of the limited consumables. The other three TELMUs, who all made significant contributions to the flight, were Jack Knight (Gold Team), Robert Heselmeyer (Maroon Team), and Bill Peters (White Team).

On April 13, 1970, the spacecraft was more than halfway to its destination, and I had just arrived on shift and was getting my handover briefing from the outgoing TELMU when those now-infamous words from astronaut Jack Swigert sent a jolt through the control room: "Houston, we've had a problem here." On board the spacecraft, the red master alarm light flashed, and a main bus under voltage indicated a serious issue in the Command Module. Cap Com Jack Lousma, not quite certain what the crew had said, called out, "This is Houston. Say again, please." This time it was Lovell who called down from the CSM: "Houston, we've had a problem. We've had a Main Bus B undervolt."[3]

In the control room, four rows of flight controllers huddled over their consoles and watched intently to get some insight from their telemetry data. At first the data on the TV screens was scrambled, and we weren't sure if we were experiencing real problems or simply bad data. No one at that moment knew the extent of the disaster that had just occurred. Because sound waves don't travel in space, the crew had not heard the extent of the violent explosion that had just ripped out the side of their spacecraft. Initially, they thought perhaps they had been struck by a meteorite, and at once Jack Swigert began trying to install the hatch between the CSM and the LM, which was like trying to isolate a leak in a submarine. Little did they know that the leak was in their mothership. Installing the hatch proved to be difficult, as it had about a dozen latches that needed to be secured for installation. After a few minutes, Swigert abandoned the task. This turned out to be somewhat of a miracle in itself, because if he had indeed installed the hatch, and then later had to remove it, the extra time would have eaten into the life of both the oxygen supply and the CSM batteries, which had seriously degraded.

After several minutes, EECOM Sy Liebergot finally surmised that something dreadfully serious had happened that had impacted oxygen tanks 1 and 2 as well as affected the fuel cells. Main electrical bus B was under voltage, and fuel cells 1 and 3 were down. Oxygen pressure from oxygen tank 2 was reading zero, and the other tank was dropping. The bad thing about losing oxygen was that it was not only the primary source of breathable atmosphere for the crew but also provided power to the fuel cells, which were the primary power source for the CSM. The scenario was something like we had never seen before, something Sy Liebergot later said appeared to be a quadruple failure.

EECOM soon reported that oxygen tank 1 was still leaking and at that rate would be lost in less than two hours. The situation was bleak and getting bleaker. With the reality of the loss of both oxygen tanks and the loss of the primary power system, we quickly realized that we had lost our mission to the Moon and, more important, we would soon be fighting just to keep the crew alive. The obvious immediate choice was to power up the Lunar Module to buy some time. With the Black Team taking over, Flight Director Gene Kranz and the White Team moved downstairs in the Mission Control Center complex to work problems as a "tiger team," looking at how to manage the power usage and various return options.

As Glynn Lunney and the Black Team took control, our entire team was thoroughly immersed in several problems. Glynn handled the situation masterfully, however. In fact, Ken Mattingly later said of Glynn, "No general or admiral in wartime could ever be more magnificent than Glynn was that night. He and he alone brought all of the scared people together."[4]

The next miracle, really, was powering up the LM itself in midflight to serve as a lifeboat. The LM was designed with an independent power system for lunar landings, but we didn't have immediate procedures for that sort of operation. Our TELMU team quickly tackled the task of coming up with an appropriate procedure to power up the LM, as it wasn't just a simple task of turning it on with a single switch throw. Equipment had to be turned on in a certain sequence and control gained in the LM, or we risked the chance of turning our only batteries offline and losing altitude control. Then all would be lost. Again, the importance of teamwork was a critical factor. I worked with the Control Team to shorten the procedures that normally would take two hours to complete. However, the time crunch of getting the LM powered up was coming into play. When the EECOM announced that we only had thirty minutes remaining, we knew we had to hurry. Fred Haise had already headed into the

LM with a flashlight. We went ahead and instructed the crew to turn on the LM's oxygen supply. The CSM oxygen supply was dwindling fast as we voiced the power-up procedure. Although time was running out, we knew we had to keep the power going, since it was of critical importance to transfer the CSM's inertial guidance alignment to the LM's computer. We were down to the final minutes of remaining oxygen when the last computer transfers were made.

At 10:50 p.m. local Houston time, about an hour and a half into our shift, the CSM was powered down. The CSM was now lifeless, destined to be a cold, clammy pit. Unfortunately, about 20 amp-hours of entry battery power (about 15 percent) had been used before the CSM was powered down.

After *Aquarius* (nickname for the LM) was successfully powered up, we spent the next suspenseful minutes calculating the available LM life support consumables—power, water, and oxygen. We faced the seemly impossible task of making the LM lifeboat, which was designed for two men for only a day or two, last for three men for almost four days. As it turned out, we had enough oxygen because of the planned re-pressurizations on the lunar surface, but power and water (which was needed to cool the equipment) would run out long beforehand. Early estimates at current power rates showed us running short of power by some thirty-six hours. Our initial estimates of consumable usage were so concerning that some team members wanted to turn the CSM around immediately and perform what was known as a direct abort with the CSM engine.

There was considerable discussion of this option along with the other major option, which would use the LM engine to send the combined LM/CSM spacecraft toward the Moon in a slingshot maneuver. This approach would then hurl the combined LM/CSM back toward the Earth using the Moon's gravity. This would take a little longer but would fire the LM descent engine instead of the CSM's engine. In another miracle, the team decided not to use the CSM engine as it would most likely fail. In fact Gene Kranz himself said, "Through some miracle, a burst of intuition, something we had all seen, heard, or felt now told us, 'Don't use the main engine.' To this day I still can't explain why I felt so strongly about that option."[5] To this day I still believe a higher power was guiding us.

The next difficult challenge was to reconfigure the LM to a lower power and water usage rate. Even at lower rates, our TELMU calculations showed that we would run out of power some twenty hours early and run out of water thirty-six hours early. It appeared that water was the limiting consumable. Unless the vehicle was cooled, its equipment would fail. Some flight controllers and engineers were strongly arguing for the computer and other equipment to be kept online to keep the inertial guidance intact and avoid jeopardizing additional rocket burns yet to come. Our data, however, showed that if we didn't power down to a much lower level, we wouldn't make it. We needed to turn almost everything off—even computers and navigation equipment.

The urgency of the situation led me to take drastic action to make our point heard. Breaking with the standard voice protocol of talking to the Flight Director over the voice intercom system, I unplugged my headset, walked up to the Flight Director station (only a few feet away), and talked with Glynn Lunney directly. I knew he was a perceptive and responsible engineer, and I felt that he respected my opinion. I said, "Glynn, if we don't get this thing powered down, we're not going to make it." He nodded his head and said, "Okay, let's see your data." The data indicated that we would still run out of water early even at some of the lower power levels projected.

After seeing our data, Lunney understood the situation but struck for a compromise that would keep the navigation equipment online until after the PC + 2 burn. The White Team, which included our TELMU, Bill Peters, and EECOM, John Aaron, was also working on power-down scenarios in conjunction with plans for the PC + 2 burn. Gene Kranz was adamant that the inertial guidance system remain online until after the PC + 2 burn, and then we would power down to a bare minimum. So the compromise plan would power down the LM from 32 to 25 amps after the free return burn at 61:30 mission elapsed time, but keep the guidance system online until after the PC + 2 burn. Then, after the PC + 2 burn, virtually everything would be shut down. Although it didn't guarantee success, the plan

APOLLO 13—THE REST OF THE STORY

inserted a degree of hope into the situation; the odds of whether we would make it were still too close to call. The plan was voiced to the crew, and about five and a half hours after the accident, a successful free-return burn was performed by the LM descent engine, which propelled the astronauts and our lifeboat around the far side of the Moon and then earthward.

At 9:00 a.m. my shift was over. We handed over responsibility to Flight Director Gerry Griffin and the Gold Team. I'll never forget that day (or night). It had been the busiest shift our whole team had ever experienced at NASA. Our team was ushered into a press room where the rest of the world was just waking up and wanted to hear the story. Although exhausted, we tried to explain what had happened and the status of the crew. As engineers, we had done the best we could, but would it be enough? Back in the control center, I prayed that the Lord would guide us and that we as flight controllers would not make any mistakes in our actions that would jeopardize the safe return of the crew.

As I drove home, the events of the preceding traumatic hours revolved in my head. At home I turned on the TV, and there to my surprise was CBS anchor Walter Cronkite relaying our story to a waiting world. Flipping through the local papers, I saw articles and cartoons illustrating the world's compassion and interest in our unfolding Apollo drama. One of the surprising things that happened was the tremendous outpouring of prayer all across the country and even worldwide. Special prayer vigils were called. The Pope issued a proclamation that all people should pray. Even the US Senate passed a resolution that all people should go to their churches and synagogues or pause and pray for the safe return of the three astronauts. I too prayed for the three men as their lives hung in the balance. Like so many others around the world, I asked God to stretch the consumables for their return like Christ himself had done some 2,000 years ago when he took the bread and two fish and fed at least 5,000 people.

During this period, it seemed that as we got one problem under control a new one would crop up. When the Gold Team took over, the team faced another problem for the PC + 2 burn. Normally the navigation alignment would be made using the LM's Alignment Optical Telescope (AOT) to fix on a particular star, somewhat like an ancient mariner of old. The problem now was that, since the explosion, hundreds of pieces of debris were hovering around the spacecraft, and when we used the AOT, it was fooled into thinking the debris were stars. Guidance officer Ken Russell came up with the alternate solution of using the biggest star in the star field, the Sun. Although the alignment with the Sun wouldn't be as precise as that with a distant star, and the crew would have to maneuver the vehicle into position for the reading, there was no better option. Although Lovell had his doubts while discussing the procedure with Haise, the option was tested in the simulator, and it proved to be feasible.[6] The procedure was voiced to the crew, and they performed the update. The Sun update didn't work as well as a star sighting, but it worked well enough. I later marveled at the precise design of the universe and the incomparable laws and geometry that allowed us to make such calculations.

After the PC + 2 burn, the faithful LM was powered down to a bare minimum, just around 15 amps of power—whereas normally we ran around 55 amps. Rick Houston reported in his book *Go Flight!*: "That was not belt tightening, that was noose strangling."[7] Bob Heselmeyer, our Maroon Team TELMU, chuckled and said, "There wasn't that much powered up, but what was powered up, I can guarantee you, was watched very carefully."[8]

It wasn't long after our power profile was stabilized that several other problems began to surface. With three men in the close quarters of the cabin, the crew's breathing slowly began poisoning the cabin atmosphere with carbon dioxide. Our system for carbon dioxide removal provided for the cabin air to flow through a lithium hydroxide canister. Again, due to the lunar landing flight plan, we only had enough replacement canisters in the LM to last a day or two, and then the crew would suffocate. We did have Command Module replacement canisters, but they were square and our LM container was round. It was like trying to put a square peg in a round hole. You probably know the story of how Ed Smylie and the crew systems team went to work designing a makeshift container out of checklist

APOLLO 13—THE REST OF THE STORY

cardboard, a stowage bag, duct tape, and air hoses, attempting a fix before sharing it with the astronauts.

By midmorning, the crew systems engineers reviewed the fix with our TELMU team and Ken Mattingly. It looked good to us, and, just as the carbon dioxide buildup was reaching unacceptable levels of some 7.5 mmHg in the LM, Cap Com Joe Kerwin voiced up the lengthy procedure on how to fabricate the makeshift container and hook it to the existing system. About a half hour after the fix was in place, the carbon dioxide reading was down to 0.3 mmHg. It worked! Again, a miracle.

What you may not know is that in addition to the team working on the makeshift fix, several people on the ground were praying for help. There was an interesting incident of a Christian lady who lived in nearby Dickenson and had a farm. That night she had a dream that she was trying to get a large pig into a square pen. She and her crew worked and finally got the pig in the pen. When she heard of our dilemma, she prayed for some way for us to get that round peg (the lithium hydroxide canister) into a square container. I believe there were men on our team who felt the inspiration of those prayers and came up with a makeshift way to make it work.

As the CSM/LM continued its journey and got closer to Earth, it was noticed that the vehicle trajectory was still too shallow (although not known at the time, the cooling vapor from the LM sublimator was venting, causing a slight thrust to the vehicle and throwing it off course). During the reentry phase only the Command Module (then separated from the Service Module) would enter the Earth's atmosphere. If its entry angle was too shallow, it would skip on the atmosphere like a rock with no chance for recovery. Another burn was needed, but now no help from the LM's guidance system was available since powering up that system and the computer would use too much electrical power. As it turned out, there was a little-known backup procedure that required using the Earth's limb (horizon) and pointing the vehicle in a manual or "dead reckoning" approach. The vehicle would have to be maneuvered to the correct altitude and the engine started and stopped manually, based on Mission Control's prescribed time for its operation.

A few years earlier, prior to *Apollo 8*, a TRW engineer had developed a backup program to compute this type of burn; however, it required extensive crew training and know-how. But once again God was guiding. Of all the astronauts in the astronaut core, only one had trained on this procedure in flight. Fortuitously, Jim Lovell had experimented with the procedure on *Apollo 8*, and it had worked. So the crew was given the "Go" to use the procedure again. They maneuvered the spaceship to get a fix on Earth's limb. There was still concern about whether the LM engine would perform adequately. Bill Stoval, the Guidance Officer (GUIDO), did not know if the thrust profile in the Mission Control Center would match the thrust profile when the engine started.[9] The burn time was voiced up to the crew, and Swigert covered the timing with a stopwatch. The midcourse correction burn was made, and it went off perfectly.

As soon as we got these problems sorted out, another problem stared us in the face. It had been determined that the Command Module batteries, which were required for reentry, had been severely degraded during the final minutes of transfer after the explosion. As it stood, there wasn't adequate power to last through the entry phase, and with the fuel cells inoperable for charging, it looked like an impossible situation. But God had other plans. Art Campos, the LM power engineer, also a Christian, was at home when he heard of the dilemma. Coincidently, he had gone to see the movie *Marooned* on the evening of April 13, and in the movie "charging" of the batteries was required to fix a certain problem. Later that night, Campos was awakened by a phone call informing him that the *Apollo 13* spacecraft had suffered an accident and that he needed to come in and work on a way to get power to the entry batteries in the Command Module, required for reentry. Interestingly enough (although again perhaps a higher power was guiding), years before at an LM engineering design review, our own TELMU Bill Peters had come up with a design modification to the LM heater circuitry. Bill had proposed a wiring redesign so that the CSM could maintain heat in the unpowered LM during translunar coast. When the spacecrafts were designed, however, it was never envisioned that such a cable would be needed to charge the Command Module batteries from the LM.

APOLLO 13—THE REST OF THE STORY

Now, when Campos arrived at the Mission Evaluation Room, he recalled the movie, where they said "charge the batteries"—and then he remembered a procedure he had devised about a year earlier to charge the entry batteries using the heater cable between the two vehicles. Dick Brown, one of our NR support engineers, remembered the heater circuit redesign Peters had modified a couple of years earlier. Then the procedure flashed through their minds, with a configuration where the cable could be used for the battery recharging. They attempted the configuration in the simulators, but the simulator didn't allow it to work, since it only mathematically modeled the normal operations circuit. However, the procedure was tried in orbit, and it worked well. Again a miracle—more than just a fortuitous design of the LM heater circuit. With the LM batteries now coming in with a better-than-expected power margin, the CM batteries were topped off with an extra 15 percent or so on Wednesday and Thursday.

As *Aquarius* continued its dangerous journey back to Earth, still another threatening situation emerged. The weather forecasts predicted a hurricane in the Pacific Ocean right where our target landing was to be. NASA meteorologists predicted that Hurricane Helen would move into the designated *Apollo 13* landing site the day of reentry and splashdown. Talk about drama! We faced one suspenseful moment after another. The intensity and unpredictability of the storm made selection of a landing site difficult for the Retrofire officer. No reentry had ever landed in a tropical storm, and *Apollo 13* might be the first. If the vehicle splashed down amid a storm, the capsule might drift and be lost at sea. To conserve the entry battery power, the beacon light recovery system would be deactivated and the crew would be invisible to those looking for the capsule bobbing up and down in the Pacific Ocean. They would eventually have to blow the hatch, and the *Apollo 13* capsule could possibly sink, similar to Gus Grissom's *Liberty Bell*. Again, what do you do? You pray and go with your gut feeling. Because of the timing criticality of the vehicle's landing, the decision was made to ignore the weather forecasts, which ended up being a fortuitous decision because Hurricane Helen ultimately changed course.

As we approached the end of our mission, a little less than five hours before reentry, the vehicle trajectory had shallowed again, and a fifth midcourse correction burn was required. Since the LM guidance platform was still not available, the crew again had to orient the vehicle using the Earth limb terminator procedure. This time the terminator of the Earth appeared as more of a crescent moon; it was set in the crosshairs of the AOT for the alignment, and the burn was made. The final trajectory began to fall into place.

About twenty minutes after the burn, it was time to cast off the damaged Service Module. At around 7:14 a.m. local time on Friday, Jim Lovell's description of the damage sent a chill through the control room. "Okay, Houston . . . there's one whole side of that spacecraft missing. Right by the . . . Look out there, will you? Right by the high-gain antenna, the whole panel is blown off, almost at the base of the engine." Cap Com Joe Kerwin replied, "Copy that." The base of the Service Module was close to the heat shield, and if that were damaged it could be catastrophic for the reentry. Gerry Griffin said, "We figured there had been some kind of damage, but we didn't know how extensive. At that point there wasn't much you could do about it."[10]

Haise continued, "Yes, it looks like it got the SPS [CSM main engine] bell too . . . . It's really a mess." Again, how fortunate that Kranz and the team decided to go with the LM engine instead of the CSM for the burn, as who knows what would have happened otherwise.[11]

On April 17, the modules were back in the Earth's sphere of influence, and it was time to power up the CM module. As Jack Swigert floated back into his once-familiar cockpit, the inside of the *Odyssey* (CM nickname) was like a cold, clammy tin can. Everything was covered or soaked with moisture. His immediate concern was that with all the moisture on the outside of the controls, there might also be moisture on the underside that had seeped into electrical harnesses and switches, which would lead to short circuits when it was powered up. All he could do was hope and pray. Again, miracle of miracles, as the switches were thrown the reentry batteries took over and brought the CM back to life without any issues. The

APOLLO 13—THE REST OF THE STORY

CM platform was aligned based on the LM's alignment, using the same technique used much earlier to transfer the CSM alignment to the LM.

Next it came time to jettison our faithful *Aquarius*. It was a vehicle that could never have flown in the Earth's atmosphere, yet it had faithfully done its job as a lifeboat. I think our whole TELMU team was on shift for the jettison. It was sort of a happy, excited time, a time of elation, as we felt that our TELMU team had done its part to save the mission as well as the lives of the astronauts. As with life itself, however, we were excited and ready to move on to the next stage to see if the Command Module could withstand the stress of reentry. So, at 10:53 a.m. Friday morning Houston time, *Aquarius* was separated and sent on its way with a note of thanks and a final farewell.

At 142 hours, 40 minutes, and 46 seconds into the flight, around 1:53 p.m. local time on Friday, April 17, the crew successfully fired its retro rockets, which plunged the vehicle into the Earth's atmosphere. Again, the whole team was present for the landing. At this point, all we could do was pray and hope that the heat shield would do its job. In Gene Kranz's book *Failure Is Not an Option*, he said, "We were now in the hands of God and a deadly tired crew executing a set of procedures written on scraps of paper in the Command Module, procedures that had not existed eighteen hours ago."[12] After a few minutes, the vehicle went into communications blackout, and the control room was absolutely silent. When we didn't hear them at the expected time, there were more anxious moments. Some were thinking there had been some damage to the heat shield and that we had lost our crew. After about an agonizing minute and a half past the anticipated time of blackout end, voice contact came.

Cap Com Joe Kerwin called, "*Odyssey*, Houston, standing by. Over." A few seconds passed and the voice of Swigert came back: "OK, Joe." Shortly thereafter, we saw the three large orange and white parachutes on our giant TV screens. The control room erupted with cheers and the waving of American flags. The crew landed right in the prescribed location in the Pacific, and there was no hurricane.

It had miraculously moved out of range. The crew was quickly recovered by the recovery team and safe at last.

As I mentioned at the beginning of this chapter, for me the flight of *Apollo 13* was not a failure but a flight of miracles. It seemed that we had been part of an impossible journey. One could argue the reality of the miracles I have attested to, and give all the credit to ingenious design or the engineering prowess of savvy flight controllers. (Again, I'll discuss the possibility of miracles in the next chapter.) But for me, the timing of certain events (e.g., Lovell's earlier training for the navigation update procedure and the inability to install the LM hatch early on) and the sheer magnitude of fortuitous decisions that were made (e.g., the heater cable design before the flight, the decision not to use the CSM engine, ignoring the meteorology predictions for landing), coupled with the catastrophic things that could have happened if events were slightly different, were more than luck or coincidence. Consider the fact of what other scenarios would have led to. If the explosion had occurred on the CSM *after* the lunar landing or, worse yet, while the LM was on the Moon, results would have been entirely different.

Those of us who worked in the MOCR for that perilous flight were privileged to be part of history that shaped our lives. For me, it was a hinge on which my life has turned. I believe God used the events of *Apollo 13* to reveal himself to me and provide a door through which I entered into theological dimensions. In the following chapters I'll share some of those thoughts. Although I didn't realize it at the time, God was calling me, prodding me, to get to know him at a much deeper level.

Notes

1. Rick Houston and Milt Heflin, *Go Flight! The Unsung Heroes of Mission Control, 1965-1992* (Lincoln: University of Nebraska Press, 2015) 199.

2. Ibid., 199.

3. Ibid., 208.

4. Ibid., 221.

5. Eugene F. Kranz, *Failure Is Not an Option* (New York: Simon & Schuster, 2000) 317.

6. Houston, *Go Flight!* 232.

7. Ibid., 234.

8. Ibid.

9. Ibid., 237.

10. Ibid., 242.

11. Kranz, *Failure Is Not an Option*, 334.

12. Ibid., 335.

Chapter 4

Sensing Spiritual Realities in a Physical World

Seeing the Son

After *Apollo 13*, four more Apollo flights successfully launched from planet Earth, and four more Lunar Modules touched down on lunar soil. I was fortunate to participate as the LM TELMU in all of them. They were more robust than earlier flights in the sense that the LM was outfitted with a Lunar Roving Vehicle (LRV) for *Apollo 15–17*, and the astronauts explored larger expanses of the lunar landscape, collected a multitude of lunar samples, and left a number of scientific instruments. These flights, along with Skylab and the shuttle and space station programs, have been well documented in books and other media, so I want to turn now to another dimension of life— that which we call "spiritual." It is a dimension we cannot see with our physical eyes but one that some would claim is more real than the physical.

From a larger perspective, we ask, "How does God reveal himself to us?" More fundamentally, assuming there is a supreme being, how does he reach out and make himself known to us? Does God communicate with us through the marvel of the universe? Do miracles really happen? Perhaps even more profoundly, how do we even know the spiritual dimension is real?

We hear a lot about miracles today, and there is a large volume of work addressing the subject—more than I could address in this book. In my experience of *Apollo 13*, I felt moved in a special way by what I felt was answered prayer and the miraculous recovery of the crew. As I mentioned in the last chapter, far too many unique circumstances and extraordinary events fell into place and demonstrated that a higher power was protecting us. Miracles—or even unexplained circumstances that coincidently happen in congruence with our need—testify to a supernatural working and the answers to prayer. Sometimes circumstantial events happen: a phone call, a chance meeting, an unexpected bonus check, a song on the radio, or a word from a friend just when we needed something. These things stir us, speak to us, and, at a deeper level, cause us to sense that perhaps God is revealing himself to us.

God often uses "supernatural" workings or circumstantial events to speak to us. In a technical sense, some of these things may not be defined as miracles—such as the design of the LM heater circuitry years earlier, the fortuitous training of Jim Lovell in the use of a backup navigation procedure, or even the extremely providential movement of a hurricane away from a predesignated landing area. We might call these acts of providence, whereby God is simply orchestrating natural events—not suspending the natural but controlling the natural so that it does what he wants it to do. However, I believe these supernatural acts demonstrate a loving and compassionate God reaching out to us to make himself known.

A miracle might then be defined as an extraordinary event wrought by God that cannot be explained by any natural means. It is where the laws of nature are seemingly violated or suspended and there is no physical or scientific explanation. This is when fuel cell pressure increases even though the physical environment demands a decrease by natural law. This is when a cancerous tumor mysteriously goes into remission or seemingly vanishes without medical explanation. These things get our attention and testify to a supernatural power. There are numerous miracles recorded in the Bible and many more documented in history. The crossing of the Israelites through the Red Sea led by Moses in the Old Testament or the feeding of five thousand with two fish and five loaves of bread by Jesus are two striking examples. Miracles play a particularly powerful role in Christianity, especially the most significant miracle of all—Christ's resurrection from the dead.[1]

One might then ask why God doesn't use miracles more frequently to reveal himself. C. S. Lewis wrote, "God does not shake miracles into nature at random as if from a pepper-caster. They come on great occasions and are found at the great ganglions of history—not political or social history, but of that spiritual history which cannot be fully known by men."[2] I believe that the way God works in the world is not normally by breaking the laws of nature but by quietly attracting individuals through his compassion, truth, goodness, awe, and redemptive spirit as revealed in numerous ways discussed in this chapter. John Polkinghorne makes this point: "Miracles are not to be interpreted as divine acts against the laws of nature (for those laws are themselves expressions of God's will) but as more profound revelations of the character of the divine relationship to creation."[3] In other words, because of God's great desire to relate to and rescue humanity, he sometimes reaches beyond the wall of physical barriers and touches the heart of a hurting soul; in doing so, he reveals his great love for all people.

I would also agree that miracles require an element of faith. Faith is one of those spiritual qualities that goes beyond the physical realm and bears witness to the soul. According to noted theologian Bruce Epperly, "Faith opens us to new dimensions of reality and within these new dimensions, miraculous releases of divine energy, congruent with the laws of nature, are released."[4] Faith is believing without seeing—or perhaps a different way of seeing. Faith helps us believe without having any proof other than the changed lives of the individuals involved. Faith is a way that God reaches out to touch the depths of our soul. But faith is not necessarily "blind." It is based on the traces of God's image and power he has left for us in the universe and the world around us. I believe God intentionally leaves traces and clues and acts in providential ways to lead us to faith. God's design and purpose have been woven into the fabric of history.

Dr. Bill Nichols says in his book *Healthy Faith*,

> A healthy faith is based on reliable evidence, not wishful thinking, superstitions, myths or fairytales. It's founded on time-tested, trustworthy findings including a real, personal God who acted in real historical events and in real people's lives. Your faith is not healthy because of bright ideas, the latest fad, or popular theory, but because of solid research and dependable evidence.[5]

Several of the astronauts and ground controllers bore witness of this kind of faith and were touched in a special way by the awe and inspiration of their Apollo experiences. A prime example is Colonel Jim Irwin. Jim flew as the LM Pilot on *Apollo 15* and touched down in the hilly region of Hadley Rille, a valley on the Moon. Of all the people who walked on the Moon, Jim probably had the most profound spiritual experience. In the documentary *In the Shadow of the Moon*, David Sington says Jim "had a 'road to Damascus' experience on the moon."[6]

As Jim Irwin stood on the lunar surface, with sunlight reflecting off the landscape, God's words came to him from the book of Psalms: "I look unto the hills from whence cometh my help" (121:1). Jim sensed God's help and strength, and by faith he felt God reaching out to him. He felt the mysterious presence of a spiritual force. The beauty of the mountains of the Moon moved Jim, and he said he experienced the presence of God as he never had before. In his book, *To Rule the Night*, Jim Irwin describes his spiritual experience:

> I felt an overwhelming sense of the presence of God on the moon. The ultimate effect was to deepen and strengthen all the religious insight I ever had. It remade my faith. I had become a skeptic about getting guidance from God, and I know I had lost the feeling of His nearness. On the moon the total picture of the power of God and His Son Jesus Christ became abundantly clear to me. I felt His spirit more closely than I have ever felt it on the earth, right there beside me—it was amazing.[7]

Some people would consider a trip to the Moon as one of humankind's greatest accomplishments, but Irwin had a different perspective. Afterward, he frequently said, "I believe Jesus Christ walking on the earth is more important than man walking on the moon."[8] Irwin retired from NASA in 1972 and founded High Flight, a Christian ministry. He traveled frequently and spoke to groups about the ways his experiences in space increased his awareness of the presence of God. Irwin's striking picture of himself with the lunar hills in the background along with the quote from Psalms printed on that photo hangs in my office today.

Other astronauts such as John Glenn, who was the first American to orbit the Earth and later flew on space shuttle *Discovery*, were also significantly touched by what they saw. Onboard the *Discovery* on November 1, 1998, Glenn broadcast down, "I don't think you can be up here and look out the window as I did the first day and see the earth from this vantage point, to look out at this kind of creation and not believe in God. To me, it's impossible . . . it just strengthens my faith. I wish there were words to truly describe what it's like . . . truly awesome."[9]

In my case, the inspiring events of *Apollo 13* profoundly affected my life and led me to take a different turn. I somehow felt called to probe into a deeper look at God and theological studies even though I didn't know at the time what direction that would go. Although a Christian, I had faced serious conflicts between what I was taught about the Bible and undeniable scientific discoveries. Because of what I had seen and experienced with *Apollo 13*, I felt compelled to pursue the truths about God and science and how to integrate the two. It seemed to me that a God who had the compassion to reach out and save the lives of three astronauts, and who claimed to be the Creator of the universe, was big enough to resolve any issue between science and faith. The great Creator is also the great Integrator of one world.

Also because of God's great desire to unify and restore humanity, I believe one of the spiritual realities God imparts to us is a spirit of "peace." It's an intangible quality that testifies to a higher power. As I mentioned to Rick Houston and as he recorded in his book *Go*

Flight, although there were clearly uncertainties about the future in the *Apollo 13* flight, I had a sense of peace: "There was a feeling of, 'I don't know how it's going to happen.' There was certainly a feeling of not knowing. You can only do so much. You pray, you do what you can do, which is what we did, and leave the rest up to God. I sort of felt all along that they would get back, that God would work it out. I never had the feeling of hopelessness or depression."[10] Because of this underlying peace, I felt that God was guiding us and that any issue of scientific truth and biblical truth could be resolved.

Concerning the fundamental questions on sensing spiritual realities, let us consider these ideas more deeply along with, in a broader sense, the study of God, or theology. Theology or spiritual study, like science, is also a search for truth. It is what drives us to explore the unknown. Theology is a search for truth in our understanding of God and how he relates to humanity and the world. Science is an objective study to explore and understand our physical world and the universe. We explore the universe with our five senses, whereas spiritual entities are in a different dimension, a different sense or reality not perceived with our natural senses. Of course, God's domain is both the physical and the spiritual world. But as distinguished scientist Francis Collins notes, the spiritual world is a realm not really possible to explore with the tools and language of science or with our five senses; it must be examined with the heart, the mind, and the soul, and ultimately accepted by faith. Collins says that in his search for truth he came to the conclusion that if God exists, he must exist outside the natural world, and as such the tools of science are not the right ones to use when we want to learn about God.[11]

I'd also like to point out that the existence of God and spiritual reality can never be proved by scientific discovery. There are certainly credible scientists who are atheists. Some see God in the handiwork of the created universe, and some do not. There may be traces of the spiritual and unexplained miraculous events that seemingly point to something more than can be explained with scientific methods, but they are often hard to repeat. There may be scientific wonders and miraculous events that awe and inspire, but the mind must find a way to embrace both the spiritual and the physical. However, these traces of God's activity that often inspire us and engender a spirit of wonder can also drive us on a quest to probe deeper into God's mysterious being.

In his Regent's Study Guide *In the Beginning God*, John Weaver says that there is an important difference between the place of experience in science and its place in theology. Science can repeat experiments in order to recreate experiences, but Christian experience is personal, and each instance often has its own uniqueness. Yet there is still something universal about the character of spiritual experiences, since people exist in relation with each other.[12] I have seen the Christian experience in others' lives played out in love and kindness to fellow human beings, which gives credence to the idea that their lives were touched by something more than a myth. I would agree with John Polkinghorne, who points to the Christian experience as one of the strongest indicators of the validity of the claim that religion (spiritual truth) is in touch with reality.[13] I personally sensed the awesomeness and fingerprint of God through a number of avenues: through the beauty and wonder of the cosmos, through the miracles of *Apollo 13*, through learning of God's character in Scripture, and through seeing God's presence lived out in the lives of others.

Just as physical perceptions of mass and density can be identified, I believe spiritual perceptions and experiences can also be identified. I would list such experiences of conversion, inspiration, guidance, prayer, miracles, and worship as valid and common to those who claim spiritual experiences. They are substantiated with feelings and attitudes of joy, love, hope, kindness, peace, faith, purpose, and wholeness. These feelings may not happen in a uniform way to everyone, but they have common characteristics whenever they happen. A sense of reality, a sense of emotion and conviction, tugs at your heart. It is so real and powerful that you are moved to belief and action.

There are several contributors to the revelation of God and spiritual dimensions. As I alluded to earlier, a major contributor to the revelation of God and his character is the sacred writing in the Bible. Most of what we know about Jehovah God, his character, and his revelation and movement with the Jewish people comes from the

Old Testament. Most of what we know about Jesus, his miracles and teachings, the early apostles, and the activities of the early church comes from the New Testament. Christian theology presents models of God that are largely derived from the images and metaphors in biblical accounts of people's experience of their relationship with God and his unveiling of himself to them.

Through these accounts, we learn of God's relational character and his desire for redemption of humanity. In fact, it is primarily in the teachings of Jesus that we learn that God is more than a divine Creator who stands aloof in the heavens; rather, God wants to be in relationship with us—a "Father" to us. Of course, this raises the issue of the source and acceptance of the Bible as reliable and accurate or a work full of myths and stories.[14] Suffice it to say that the Holy Text was written by more than forty different authors over a period of some 1,500 years, yet it offers a picture of God's character and activities in the world in a unified manner. The authors of the various books wrote in different places and in three different languages. Additionally, although the Bible deals with many controversial subjects in ancient times, there is still unity along with application to our lives today.

Another of the most common ways in which God reveals himself is through other people and their spoken or written words. Certainly, many a soul has been stirred and brought to conviction or simply heard a word of comfort or guidance through the words of others. I believe that in some mysterious way, God's Spirit enlivens or touches the spirit in another individual through what others say about God. In fact, in the Bible (John 4), when Jesus speaks with a Samaritan woman one day, he tells her that true worship with God comes through "Spirit and truth." In other words, revelation of truth often comes to us through the Holy Spirit and through the truth that is communicated by others in a worship experience. In a sense, our spirits and minds are inspired by God's Spirit, and truth is revealed to us. It's like a "eureka" moment when the light comes on.

What I consider a major contributor in God's revelation, and what I plan to discuss more fully in the next chapter, comes to us through science. As I mentioned above, although science may not answer ultimate questions about the reality and character of God, I believe it has much to show us about God and spiritual realities. In fact, science is presenting an ever-clearer picture of the universe and how it testifies to a divine being. As we seek the truth, the universe overwhelms us with a sense of mystery and awe. As we look at the starry heavens and consider the study of cosmology or look at the genius of subatomic electron flow, we get a new appreciation of God's revelation. Whether we study the macro level or the micro level, whether cosmology or biology, we see God's fingerprint. Whether we study the Milky Way, the human genome, the petal of a flower, a snowflake, the intricacies of the atom, or the nature of light, they all testify to a divine mind that lies behind them. In many cases, these facts are just now becoming evident. And the more we look, the more we see that the cosmos gushes forth with knowledge.

I believe that above all of these types of revelation, the incarnation of God in Christ supremely points to God's character and his relationship with the world. As I will discuss in the chapters ahead, although we can be exposed to the revelation of God through the majesty and design of the universe, it is ultimately Christ and the Holy Spirit that make the Father known to us. As it says in Colossians 1:15-16, "He (Christ) is the image of the invisible God, the firstborn over all creation. For by him all things were created; things in heaven and on earth, visible and invisible, whether thrones or powers or rulers or authorities; all things were created by him and for him."

As a friend of mine pointed out recently, the anomaly of Christ cannot be explained. A Christian friend, Chriold Epp, with whom I worked at NASA and who was previously a physics professor, once encountered a Christian and two atheistic astronomers who were having a discussion about God and the ingenious design of the cosmos. One astronomer pointed out that the universe and even life itself could have evolved from the Big Bang and a bunch of hydrogen and helium atoms. Chriold asked, "What, then, do you do with the person of Christ?" The astronomer quickly replied, "Well, that's the problem—all of this could be explained by a bunch of atoms, but Christ is the one anomaly."

I agree. I believe that Christ himself walked the Earth in the first century, gave us a picture of God, and somehow reveals himself to us today in a personal way, and we sense his Spirit. We come to know and experience him, perhaps through what we have learned from Scripture and science, and our "spiritual eyes" are opened. As Christ touches us through what is called the miracle of the "new birth," something in our souls is made alive to spiritual truths, and we come to know the Father in a deeper way. For me personally, as I ploughed deeper into Scripture to reconcile the Bible with the science I knew, Christ himself and the character of the Father became more real to me. I realized that God is an awesome, loving being who places great value on humanity.

It is kind of like flying on the Apollo spacecraft in complete darkness behind the Moon and then breaking the lunar horizon and seeing the dazzling light of the Sun. We are blinded and dazzled at first by its brilliance. But then with a protective visor, we can make out certain features. Through special telescopes and instruments, we can even study the many mysteries of our own solar disk and how its activity affects living here on Earth. We realize that through the regenerative energies of the Sun, our planet and life itself is reborn and growth occurs. In an analogous fashion, the Bible allows us to make out and understand the features of Christ (the Son). Then, through Christ, we come to know and understand the Father, and our lives are in a sense reborn. By knowing the Father, we then come to know and understand how to truly live. In the next chapter, we will examine some of these ideas more closely.

Notes

1. Francis S. Collins, *The Language of God* (New York: Free Press, 2006) 48.

2. C. S. Lewis, *Miracles: A Preliminary Study* (New York: MacMillan, 1960) 167.

3. John C. Polkinghorne, *Science & Theology: An Introduction* (Minneapolis: Fortress Press, 1998) 93.

SENSING SPIRITUAL REALITIES IN A PHYSICAL WORLD

4. Bruce Epperly, "Adventures in a World of Scarcity," Lectionary Readings for Pentecost, http://www.patheos.com/blogs/livingaholyadventure/2013/05/the-adventurous-lectionary-pentecost-3/.

5. Bill Nichols, *Healthy Faith* (San Bernardino CA: GWN Publishing, 2016) 4.

6. D. Sington, *In the Shadow of the Moon* (UK: Discovery Films, 2007).

7. James Irwin, *To Rule the Night* (Nashville: Holman Bible Publishers, 1982) 18.

8. Quoted in Sington, *In the Shadow of the Moon*.

9. Quoted in *The Hand of God* (Philadelphia & London: Templeton Foundation Press, 1999) 123.

10. Quoted in Rick Houston and Milt Heflin, *Go Flight! The Unsung Heroes of Mission Control, 1965–1992* (Lincoln: University of Nebraska Press, 2015) 224.

11. Collins, *The Language of God*, 6, 30.

12. John David Weaver, *In the Beginning God* (Oxford UK: Regents Park College in association with Smyth & Helwys Publishing, Macon GA, 1994) 9.

13. John Polkinghorne, *One World: The Intersection of Science & Theology* (London: SPCK, 1986) 29.

14. Many excellent sources on Christian apologetics speak to these issues. See, for example, *The Case for a Creator*, by Lee Strobel; *Evidence that Demands a Verdict*, by Josh McDowell; *The Language of God*, by Francis Collins; *Mere Apologetics*, by Alister McGrath.

Chapter 5

The Witness from Cosmology

"The heavens declare the glory of God."
(Psalm 19:1)

Sharon Begley said,

> The mystery of the heavens and their regularity—the cycling of
> the seasons, the rhythm of day and night—inspire a suspicion that
> we cannot be looking at some meaningless accident. How fitting,
> then, that it is in cosmology—the scientific study of the begin-
> ning and the evolution of the universe—where the stage is set for
> a historic reconciliation of these two rivals for man's awe: science
> and religion.[1]

In the last chapter, I mentioned my belief that science, and in particular the study of physics and cosmology, has a lot to say to theology
about the character of God and his work in the world. Paul Davies,
noted physicist, says,

> Something buried deep within the human psyche compels us to
> contemplate creation. It is obvious even at the casual glance that
> the universe is remarkably ordered on all scales. Matter and energy
> are distributed neither uniformly nor haphazardly, but organized

into coherent identifiable structures, occasionally with great complexity. . . . The cosmos, its awesome immensity, its rich diversity of forms, and above all its coherent unity cannot be accepted as a brute fact.[2]

The noted philosopher Immanuel Kant is often quoted as saying there were two enduring sources of wonder in his life: "the starry heavens above me and the moral law within me."[3] I would agree that as we consider the vast grandeur and ingenuity of the universe, our hearts and minds are stirred to reflect on the mystery and nature of a transcendent God.

More than three thousand years ago, the psalmist said, "The heavens declare the glory of God." In Hebrew, the language is even stronger, creating the image of God's revelation gushing forth. Amazing new discoveries about the cosmos seem to bombard us with truths about the universe faster than we can absorb them. Beautiful and intriguing images from the Hubble Space Telescope of gigantic galaxies, immense star clusters, and beautiful nebulae amaze and awe us almost daily. These striking images, splendid with color and motion, give us new glimpses into the outermost reaches of the universe. Reflection on the nature of the universe with such characteristics as beauty and grandeur prompts us to think of a marvelous God who produces life and beauty and in some sense takes his universe unto himself: "and God said, 'It is good'" (Gen 1).

For several years I lived in the hill country of central Texas. There, far away from the bright lights of the city, on many a summer night my wife and I marveled at the beauty of a starry night. There where Orion stretches so boldly over the southern sky, the overwhelming beauty of the sheer number of stars and ancient constellations speak volumes to us. With newer telescopes and the Hubble Space Telescope, we are even more amazed by the grandeur and sheer immensity of the universe. All stars are clustered together into galaxies, and each galaxy contains billions of stars. Our own Sun belongs to a cluster of some 200 billion stars called the Milky Way, which has the shape of a giant spiral. This giant spiral rotates slowly and majestically with its luminous arms trailing along like a gigantic sparkler.

THE WITNESS FROM COSMOLOGY   61

The size of an average galaxy is 600,000 trillion miles, and the average distance from one galaxy to another is 20 million trillion miles. As I mentioned in the introduction, the immense magnitude and distances of the entire universe simply overwhelm us. For example, the size of an average galaxy is some 100,000–200,000 light-years in diameter. Our nearest galactic neighbor, the Andromeda Galaxy, is more than two million light-years away. Thousands of galaxies exist within a distance of 100 million light-years from us, and many billions are within range of our largest telescopes.[4] Something about the immensity and grandeur of the universe reaches the limits of what our minds can fully comprehend. With this overflowing testimony of tremendous energy, space, and time, I sense God's creative power and omnipotence. It awes the soul and leads us to wonder about the significance and uniqueness of our humanity.

The size and scale of the universe are overwhelming, and the patterns and laws of the universe and natural world are intriguing. Science reveals to us the certainty and reliability of the operation of the universe. The laws of physics, the motion of the Sun and planets, and the processes at work in the Earth's weather system and atmosphere all seem to demonstrate the existence of a divine creator, a God of order and care. We can rendezvous two spacecraft and land on the Moon because of the predictability and reliability of the laws of flight dynamics and mechanical systems. Overall, the Apollo Program gave great satisfaction resulting from the tremendous performance of the Command and Lunar Modules that were designed and engineered to operate in the harsh environment of outer space—all under the natural laws of creation.

It is interesting that there is also an apparent randomness and unpredictable behavior of certain physical systems. At the subatomic level in particle physics, we were introduced to the quantum world by Max Planck and Werner Heisenberg. Heisenberg showed that particles in the quantum state do not have well-defined positions and behave with randomness and uncertainty. More recently it has been suggested that there is "chaos" within several physical systems that makes them far less predictable than Newtonian physics would allow.[5]

Chaos theory looks at the complex phenomena that are beyond the regularities of pure deterministic systems such as weather, fluid flow, air turbulence, and electrical activity in the brain. Although chaotic systems appear to behave in a random pattern, they nevertheless obey the overarching laws of the universe. As we come to understand the randomness and overall behavior of chaotic systems, we sense that there must be some greater force that is in control of the total system. Therefore it seems reasonable to suggest that there is a Creator God who allows certain freedom of development within independent systems but maintains overall sovereign control with the laws of the universe.

It seems, then, that science reveals to us an interplay of randomness and the necessity of controlling laws within the development and operation of the universe and points us to another aspect of God's creative character, namely freedom of choice. In other words, even the operation of chaotic systems allows us to make decisions and be creative. Whether you believe the Genesis narrative to be a literal retelling or simply an illustrative story, it appears that God gave Adam and Eve creative roles and volitional wills to make ultimate choices. Without free will, humankind would be nothing more than predetermined, preprogramed, robotic humanoids. I believe along with John Weaver that human free will and the role of chance within physical and biological processes can be seen as expressions of God's love.[6]

Another extraordinary discovery over the last seventy years is the confirmation of an expanding universe and the now prevailing cosmological model for the universe, the Big Bang theory. The Big Bang theory states that the universe began as a very hot, dense, and infinitesimally small singularity, with no stars, form, or structure. It then exploded with tremendous release of energy into the universe we have today.

Prior to the 1930s, there was a near-universal acceptance of the Steady State theory, where matter existed in an uncreated cosmos with no beginning and no end. Even Einstein supported the Steady State theory of the universe, and although his General Theory of

THE WITNESS FROM COSMOLOGY

Relativity required an expanding universe, he introduced a cosmic constant to counter the gravitational forces.

Then, around 1913, Melvin Slipher observed a shift toward the red end of the spectrum in light received from nearby galaxies. Each galaxy emits light within its own particular spectrum, and when it moves away from Earth, its color becomes redder than normal. This effect is called the redshift. Slipher observed that galaxies next to us were moving away from us at speeds up to 600 miles per second. The idea picked up steam when Ed Hubble, a famous astronomer, started confirming how fast neighboring galaxies were moving away from our own. Hubble observed that the distances to faraway galaxies were strongly correlated with their redshifts. This was interpreted to mean that all distant galaxies and clusters are moving away from our vantage point with an apparent velocity proportional to their distance. That is, the farther away they are, the faster they move away from us, regardless of their direction. In fact, other astronomers confirmed the findings and found that galaxies are moving away from our own at tremendous speeds of 150,000 miles per second. All of this suggests that the universe had a beginning. The light from these galaxies and quasars must have been traveling for several billion years, and from these findings the age of the Earth has been estimated at some 10–15 million years.

In the mid-1960s, Arno Penzias and Robert Wilson found further evidence supporting the Big Bang theory by discovering a sort of background cosmic radiation (afterglow) with the size and density that would be expected after the Big Bang. This background radiation in the universe was seen to be at one point with infinitely high energy and density. Based on the cosmic radiation background studies, the age of the universe is now estimated at 13.8 billion years. Other scientists and NASA observations have also found supporting evidence, such that now, most scientists are in agreement that the universe began as an infinitely dense, dimensionless point of pure energy. For the Christian, these findings give exciting new support not only to the idea of a beginning of the universe but also to a singularity that could be interpreted as a creative act by a Creator God. Even for nonbelieving scientists, the idea of this unique singularity poses the question of what caused the Big Bang to occur. Did the cosmos create itself from nothing? Or was it brought into existence by a creative agent? According to theology professor and acclaimed apologist Alister McGrath, the Christian doctrine of creation from nothing (*ex nihilo*) has enjoyed a new lease on life as a result of these new insights.[7]

The problem with the Big Bang is that it was a one-time event (a singularity). Although some notable scientists don't see a need for a Creator God, others see the unique correlation with biblical accounts. For example, in the 1988 bestseller, *A Brief History of Time*, author/scientist Stephen Hawking appeared to accept the role of God in the creation of the universe, but in a more recent publication, he concludes that there is no place for God in the creation and that the Big Bang was an inevitable consequence of the laws of physics. However, Nobel Prize winner Francis S. Collins states in his book *The Language of God* that the Big Bang itself seems to point strongly toward a Creator, since otherwise the question of what came before is left "hanging in the air."[8] After reviewing the complexity and implications of these findings, distinguished physicist Freeman Dyson said, "The more I examine the universe and the details of its architecture, the more evidence I find that the universe in some sense must have known we were coming."[9] Also, Arno Penzias, Nobel Prize-winning scientist who discovered the cosmic background radiation that provided strong support for the Big Bang, affirmed, "The best data we have are exactly what I would have predicted, had I had nothing to go on but the five books of Moses, the psalms, and the Bible as a whole."[10]

As I stated earlier in this book, although we can't prove the existence of God, the traces of omniscient fingerprints point to a divine Creator. The energy and timescale of such events as the universe's beginnings boggle the mind, and to the Christian, the age of the universe and the point at which humanity came upon the scene point to a creative God of ancient existence. The universe's immense size and timescale reach the limits of what our minds can fully comprehend. When we contemplate our existence within this framework and marvel at the beauty and complexity of life, and having the

THE WITNESS FROM COSMOLOGY 65

ability to comprehend to some degree this complexity, we sense that there is some larger purpose to it all. Perhaps we were just meant to be here. I agree with John Weaver, who says, "To the eye of faith the history of the universe is pointing to a God who does not work by magic, but who has been patiently at work over a long period of time in an evolving cosmos."[11] Here is a picture of the long, patient, and redeeming work of a compassionate God who is not willing that any should perish.

Now that the origin of the universe and our own solar system has become more understood, a number of fascinating facts about the universe and the natural world have been discovered that puzzle scientists and theologians alike. According to several scientists (e.g., Francis Collins, Stephen Hawking, and Lee Smolin), over the last few decades there has been a growing realization of the extraordinary degree of fine-tuning of the initial conditions of the Big Bang that was necessary for planets, heavy elements, and complex life even to develop at all. The way in which the universe expanded after the Big Bang depended critically on how much total mass and energy the universe had and also on the strength of the gravitational constant. In the early expansion of the universe, there had to be an extremely close balance between the expansive energy (driving things apart) and the force of gravity (pulling things together). If expansion dominated, then matter would fly apart too rapidly for condensation into galaxies and stars to take place. If the rate of expansion had been greater by even one part in a million, stars and planets would not have been able to form. On the other hand, if gravity dominated, the world and solar system would have collapsed upon itself again before the processes of life could take place. The incredible degree of fine-tuning of these physical constants has been the subject of wonder for many experts.[12] Theoretical physicist Lee Smolin points out,

> The existence of stars rests on several delicate balances between forces in nature. These require that the parameters that govern how strongly these forces act must be tuned just so. In many cases, a small turn of the dial in one direction or the other, results in a world not only without stars, but with much less structure than our universe.[13]

And Stephen Hawking writes,

> Why did the universe start out with so nearly the critical rate of expansion that separates models that recollapse from those that go on expanding forever, that even now, ten thousand million years later, it is still expanding at nearly the critical rate? If the rate of expansion one second after the Big Bang had been smaller by even one part in 100 thousand million million, the universe would have recollapsed before it ever reached its present size.[14]

According to many scientists, the same remarkable situation applies to the formation of heavier elements. If the strong nuclear force that holds together protons and neutrons had been even slightly weaker, then only hydrogen would have been formed in the universe. If, on the other hand, the strong nuclear force had been slightly stronger, all the hydrogen would have been converted into helium, instead of the 25 percent that occurred early in the Big Bang, thus allowing the fusion in stars to generate heavier elements. According to this remarkable observation, the nuclear force appears to be tuned just correctly to allow the formation of carbon, which is the building block for life forms on Earth.[15]

Altogether, there are some fifteen physical constants in the universe whose values are given—they simply have the value they have. This list includes such things as the speed of light, the force of gravity, the strong and weak nuclear forces in atoms, and various forces associated with electromagnetic energy. The chance that all of these constants would take on the necessary values to result in a stable universe capable of sustaining complex life forms is highly improbable. The term "anthropic principle," introduced by Brandon Carter in 1974, has been applied to this phenomenon and has come to be widely used as a way of speaking of these curious and illuminating properties of the beginning of the universe. Paul Davies says in his book *The Cosmic Blueprint*, "There is for me powerful evidence that there is something going on behind it all . . . . It seems as though somebody has fine-tuned nature's numbers to make the Universe . . . . The impression of design is overwhelming."[16] So because of this amazing fine-tuning of mass and energy of the

THE WITNESS FROM COSMOLOGY

developing universe that produced life as we know it, we sense the handiwork of a Creator God of ultimate wisdom.

In addition to the fine-tuning of the beginning of the universe, there are also a number of creative designs of our natural world that demonstrate a providential ordering and care for life to exist and flourish. Take for example the distance between Earth and the Sun. The Earth is an average of about 93 million miles from our Sun. The temperature on the surface of the sun is about 11,000 to 12,000 degrees Fahrenheit, and the heat that reaches across those 93,000 million miles to the Earth brings the right average temperature to sustain life. If only 50 degrees more or 50 degrees less of the Sun's heat reached Earth, life as we know it could not exist. Or consider the fact that the Earth is tilted at 23.5 degrees from the vertical. This curious tilt of the Earth gives us our seasons. If it were not tilted at 23.5 degrees, we would not only lose our seasons but also life itself as we know it. Without this tilt, the middle of the Earth would absorb too much of the Sun's energy, and the poles would not get enough. The vapors of the oceans would move north and south, piling up continents of ice.

Regardless of one's religious background, these findings clearly raise a number of theological implications. It seems that the discoveries of modern cosmology demonstrate that something of purpose is working, something initiated the Big Bang, and something continues to work in the universe and in our world. As John Weaver says, "We are encouraged by the discoveries of modern cosmology to consider a universe whose initial conditions were finely tuned so as to produce human life, conscious, aware, and able to contemplate the universe of which we are a part."[17]

For the Christian, these factors are not just suggestive of the existence of God but point us to reflect on the very character of God. I believe the behavior of subatomic particles and even the chaotic behavior of certain subsystems demonstrate a loving God who allows free will. I see a Creator God who is at work to continue to bring life and beauty and who cares for his creation. Although intelligent design is only a first step in a belief system, it nevertheless reflects the idea of purpose. Even Paul Davies, while remaining agnostic about the existence of God, concludes his book *The Mind of God* by stating, "What is man that we might be party to such a privilege? I cannot believe that our existence in the universe is a mere quirk of fate, an accident in history, an incidental blip in the great cosmic drama. Our involvement is too intimate. We are truly meant to be here."[18] It seems that all of this points to creative purpose and a personal God who not only created but is also involved in a complex universe.

Now that science has arrived at the concept of the Big Bang, in the next chapter I will examine the difficult question of origins and the harmonization of biblical interpretations with scientific models. I believe that we can find a harmony that satisfies our desire to make sense of our existence.

Notes

1. Sharon Begley, introduction to *The Hand of God* (Philadelphia & London: Templeton Foundation Press, 1999) 9.

2. Paul Davies, *The Cosmic Blueprint* (New York: Simon & Schuster, 1988) 3.

3. Quoted in Jeffrey G. Sobosan, *Romancing the Universe* (Grand Rapids MI: Wm. B. Eerdmans, 1999) 2.

4. Robert Jastrow, *God and the Astronomers* (New York: W. W. Norton & Company, 1992) 11.

5. See John David Weaver, *In the Beginning God* (Oxford UK: Regents Park College in association with Smyth & Helwys Publishing, Inc. Macon GA, 1994) 45.

6. Ibid., 9.

7. Alister McGrath, *A Fine-Tuned Universe* (Louisville KY: Westminster John Knox Press, 2009) 25.

8. Francis S. Collins, *The Language of God* (New York: Free Press, 2006) 77.

9. Quoted in J. Barrow and F. Tippler, *The Anthropic Cosmological Principle* (New York: Oxford University Press, 1986) 318.

10. Quoted in M. Browne, "Clues to the Universe's Origin Expected," *New York Times* 12 March 1978.

11. Weaver, *In the Beginning God*, 8.

12. Collins, *The Language of God*, 72.

13. Lee Smolin, *The Life of the Cosmos* (New York: Oxford University Press, 1997) 37.

14. Stephen Hawking, *A Brief History of Time* (New York: Bantam Books, 1998) 138.

15. Collins, *The Language of God*, 73.

16. Davies, *The Cosmic Blueprint*, 15.

17. Weaver, *In the Beginning God*, 47.

18. Paul Davies, *The Mind of God* (New York and London: Simon & Schuster, 1992) 332.

Chapter 6

Origins

"In the beginning God . . . ." (Gen 1)

> In the beginning God created the heavens and the earth. Now the earth was without form and void, darkness was over the surface of the deep, and the Spirit of God was hovering over the surface of the waters. And God said, "Let there be light," and there was light. God saw that the light was good, and he separated the light from darkness. God called the light "day" and the darkness he called "night." And there was evening and there was morning—the first day. (Gen 1:1-5)

When those words from Genesis 1 came tumbling down from the first manned spacecraft ever to venture around the Moon on Christmas 1968, there was a mystic awe. The words from an ancient writer inspired by a Creator God were spoken by three astronauts who had traveled farther from the bounds of planet Earth than humans had ever traveled. It seemed that there was a mysterious juxtaposition of ancient wisdom with modern science. For me, in a sense, it was a harmonization of ancient revelation and modern science.

In this chapter I want to give my own reflection and views on the ideas and understanding of origins and show that there can be harmony between faith and science. Of course, numerous volumes exist on this topic, and I will not attempt to repeat it all here, although my views reflect and hopefully synchronize with the views of numerous theological and scientific giants who have written on such matters. My primary intent is to demonstrate that science and faith can work together, even for the strict biblical literalist and the more liberal evolutionist.

For many people, the Genesis account of origins is a stumbling block. There are several points of intersection between science and Christian theology, which many perceive as areas of conflict. Some people abandon the faith today because they cannot reconcile the two, and their arguments often arise from differing views concerning origins. Some people reason that if science says the world and the universe were created some 14 billion years ago through evolutionary means, and this is seemingly in conflict with the Bible and the creation account presented in it, then how can one believe in the rest? Many fundamentalist and evangelical voices say that if one is an orthodox Christian with a high view of the Bible, he or she can't really believe in any form of evolution and accept alternate interpretations. On the other hand, many atheists and agnostics argue that if one believes in science and evolution, then he or she can't believe in God.

I believe that science and faith can be reconciled. Although I come from a conservative biblical background, I have learned to appreciate that I can have a high view of the Bible and also accept that God could have brought the world into existence and created life forms and human life in a variety of ways. We have to examine various interpretations of Scripture honestly, considering context and purpose. I believe Genesis was written by an ancient writer inspired by God who was striving to relate the creation story in a way that the ancient people of his own culture—as well as modern audiences— could understand God's creative word and relationship with creation. On the one hand, Genesis revealed to an ancient and polytheistic culture that the world was created and controlled by one all-powerful God rather than a crowd of competing gods. On the other hand, it speaks to us today and shows what it means to believe that behind all the phenomena of nature and the laws of science is an all-powerful, loving God who oversees all that happens. It is amazing how such ancient words about origins could be written with such simplicity and yet be profound enough to be understood by ancient hearers as well as modern people.

We must also realize that the book of Genesis was not intended to be a science textbook describing how creation occurred. Instead, it is a theological picture of creation revealing God's character and his relationship to humankind. I agree with John Weaver, who comments that the writer of Genesis does not attempt or want to explain creation; rather, he says the writer desires to evoke a sense of wonder at creation that will lead to worship and a proper relationship between human beings and their creator.[1] Weaver says that Genesis 1 is not science but a picture, a parable, a hymn, and above all a theological statement.[2] And David Atkinson says this about the writer of Genesis: "Debates that involve a scientific mechanism, such as those concerning a possible timescale, or evolution, or the Big Bang would hardly be high in his thought."[3]

Nevertheless, for those with a more fundamental, literalist view of Scripture, I think it is prudent to see that there are possible explanations of the creation account that can be harmonized with science. For example, for creationists who believe in a more recent age of the Earth (10,000 years or so) and a literal six-day creation account, one theory (Apparent Age Theory) is to suggest that since God is omnipotent, he created life and the universe as we observe it, with mature mountains and forests, and light traveling from galaxies and isotopes at various stages of radioactive decay, so that the universe appears to be much older than it was at the moment of creation (e.g., trees had rings, Adam was a mature adult). In this theory, even carbon dating techniques yield a time reference that appears to be much older than the data actually is.

Another theory is the Gap Theory, which asserts that the primeval creation of Genesis 1:1 was followed by 13 to 14 billion years of geologic history (gap), and then it became an Earth without form and void. The rest of the Genesis account follows a literal creation time line, but the historical signature (the Earth's apparent age) supports a modern scientific view. Another argument suggests that modern scientific calculations and conclusions of the Earth's age are basically wrong. They are based on incorrect assumptions and inaccuracies about radiometric half-life decay (radiometric dating measures radioactive decay in certain radioactive elements), lack of knowledge concerning the Big Bang, and other scientific dating calculations that show a much younger Earth (e.g., decay of the Earth's magnetic field, depth of lunar dust, amount of precipitation of certain minerals in the ocean).

When it comes to understanding the biblical account, we must first strive to understand the genre and context of its writing. Particularly as we consider the relationship between our understanding of scientific discoveries and the creation story in Genesis, we must look at the nature of the biblical account itself. Good Bible scholarship involves understanding whether the text should be taken literally or figuratively. I believe we can still have a high view of the Bible and respect biblical authority even if we do not take a passage literally. We see several illustrations in the Bible where the text should not be taken literally. (For example, in Matthew 18:22 Jesus says forgive someone seven times seventy. Here he does not mean we must forgive someone a literal 490 times.) Of course, with some texts it is more difficult to discern the genre and intent—and certainly Genesis 1 and 2 are among those passages, as scholars have debated them for centuries.

What is the genre of Genesis 1? Edward J. Young, the conservative Hebrew expert who reads the six days of Genesis as historical, admits that Genesis 1 is written in "exalted, semi-poetical language." On the one hand, it is a narrative that describes a succession of events using a historical expression characteristic of prose.[4] On the other hand, as many scholars have noted, Genesis 1's prose is extremely unusual. It has refrains, repeated statements that continually return as they do in a poem or a song. There are many examples, including the recurring refrain at the end of each creation day—"and God saw that it was good"—as well as ten repetitions of "God said," ten of "let there be," seven of "and it was so," and others. This is not the way someone normally writes in order to describe what has happened. Of course, those coming from a more literal understanding of Scripture find it difficult to accept a figurative or poetic understanding of Genesis 1. However, if the purpose of Scripture is to reveal God and his character, many scholars see that a more poetic or figurative interpretation is not only possible but also probable. John D. Weaver says Genesis 1 is a grand theological picture of the creation. He says it is dramatic prose—almost poetry—that carries a strong theological message. It is one part of the whole biblical story, which deals with the nature and revelation of God and his relationship to the world.[5]

Several Old Testament scholars (R. Kent Hughes, C. Westermann, and P. J. Wiseman) see a poetic, parable-type parallelism between the first three days of creation and the second three days.[6] In this perspective, they view the first three days as setting the broad canvas for creation and the second three days as a filling of the newly created Earth with the finer details of created things. It is a theological presentation as well as a historical narrative. For Wiseman, the key is found in verse 2, where the text says, "without form and void." He suggests that the first three days detail the formation of heaven and earth and the second three days reveal the occupation and inhabitation of the void. What we see in this construction is an amazing symmetry of creation.[7]

Day 1: Light/Energy   Day 4: Luminaries
Day 2: Sky/Atmosphere   Day 5: Birds and Fish
Day 3: Land/Plants   Day 6: Animals and Man

With respect to the word "day" as a literal twenty-four-hour day or some longer period, again we must look at the text and the context. The word "day" in Hebrew is *yom*, which simply means a span of time. As many fundamentalist scholars would point out, it is true that when taken with a definite article, it usually means a normal twenty-four-hour day, but on the other hand, as most scholars would agree, the context must ultimately determine the word's meaning. As noted Bible scholar and author Kent Hughes suggests, here in the immediate context, the seventh day in particular is not a twenty-four-hour day (because there is no evening and morning closure). Thus it indicates that the preceding six days should be similarly understood.[8]

Also, in the context of the description, several scholars feel that the six days could not be literal twenty-four-hour days because God didn't commission the Sun, Moon, and stars until the fourth day. The reason for not mentioning these luminaries on earlier days is perhaps a dense cloud cover (we understand there was another light source from verse 1), or maybe the parable form of text construction and the parallel comparison of filling the void are more theological than sequential. It also appears that the natural length of such things as plant growth and seed production would normally take longer than a twenty-four-hour period. For instance, on the third day, the text clearly states that the Earth "sprouted" plants, and the wording indicates that the plants grew from seeds or small seedlings. In addition, the plants produced seeds, which also make it difficult to accept a twenty-four-hour interpretation.

According to scholars like Hughes and Wiseman, the parallel day comparison construction would play out in the following manner.[9] The first day (vv. 1-5) reveals the initial explosion of the Big Bang with the creation of energy and matter. Energy here is another word or form for light. Genesis 1 could have read, "And God said, 'Let there be energy.'" This primal energy (light) was behind the mass that was the source of life. Energy (light) was spreading out at tremendous rates in every direction, and from the Earth's perspective the light was coming from various sources. The second day (vv. 6-8) explains how the atmosphere came into existence, a separation of the waters below from the waters above (from the Earth's perspective). From a scientific viewpoint, the significance is that this allowed the buildup of an oxygen-rich atmosphere, which filtered out the harmful ultraviolet radiation, thus allowing life to develop. On the third day (vv. 9-10), the waters of the Earth were drained into the oceans, and we see the emergence of dry land and the establishment of vegetation.

Then, according to Hughes and Weisman, we see in the second three days the "filling" of the heavens and the Earth that were created in the first three days. On day four (vv. 14-19), the lights of heaven were formed and commissioned by the Creator—the stars, Sun, and Moon, which are the bearers of the light that God made on the first day. In verse 14, several scholars feel that where the text reads, "let it be," this unusual construction is not a statement about creation but a statement of appearance and commissioning.[10] From a cosmological perspective, gravity condensed the matter and energy of the initial Big Bang into first-generation stars and galaxies. Some of the first-generation stars exploded and died, spewing out heavier matter into space. As second-generation stars and planets condensed in their turn, one of these (at least) became suitable for life as we know it. On day 4, then, from the Earth's perspective, the Sun, Moon, and stars were positioned and established to fill the void and provide heat and energy for life as well as markers for space and time. Also, as we learn from much of the rest of the Bible (Psalms, Job, and Isaiah), the stars are under God's control and declare his glory. So the Big Bang resulted not only in the creation of stars and planets but also in the creation of space and time. Interestingly, for thousands of years people have been using the stars to navigate their positions on Earth and in space—even the Apollo astronauts.

From what we understand about the birth of the stars and galaxies in the time following the Big Bang, we see that the cosmological account of the beginning parallels the biblical writer's theological presentation. As Weaver so aptly puts it, "Taking the fourth day in parallel to the first as a detailed expansion of it, we find that just as light precedes the 'lights' of heaven, so the energy explosion of the Big Bang precedes the formation of galactic bodies."[11]

On day 2, God divided the primeval waters by creating an expanse, which he called "heaven" or "sky," separating the water above from the waters below. Then, on the corresponding fifth day, the Earth was ready for its filling of living creatures. They were created first in the sea, progressing to the land and the air in the same way that fossil records demonstrate. This process would not have been viable until the development of an oxygen-rich atmosphere and until a protective ozone layer was in place. The seas and the sky swarmed with all kinds of living things, from mammoth whales and colorful goldfish to majestic eagles and indigo buntings. The Earth teemed with astonishing variety, beauty, and complexity, demonstrating a Creator God who loves beauty and variety and life itself.

On day 3, God caused the dry land to appear and covered it with vegetation. Then, on the corresponding sixth day, he filled it with land creatures. The wording of the text is meant to encompass every kind of terrestrial beast. God formed the world in three days, and in the three parallel days, he filled it with the majestic light of the Sun, Moon, and stars and with beautiful trees, plants, and amazing creatures of all kinds. Finally, the Earth was full and ready for the ultimate creation—that of humanity. Again, we don't know for certain the details of how God created human life, but I think there can be a harmonization of views. If one wants to believe in a theistic evolution (God using evolution to bring about humankind), that is fine. If one wants to believe in a creative view of people and individual species because of inconclusive support for evolutionary theory, that's fine as well. As noted author and pastor Tim Keller teaches, belief in evolution as a biological process is not the same as belief in evolution as a worldview that leads to naturalism.[12]

I personally still hold to a historical Adam and Eve, because the New Testament, namely Paul in Romans 5, teaches us that they were real in his discussion of the fall of humankind. Again, as Keller says, "Belief in evolution can be compatible with a belief in a historical faith and a literal Adam and Eve."[13] Those who believe in evolution and that Adam and Eve were not historical figures view the Adam and Eve narrative as an allegory or a symbol of the human race and feel that a doctrine of sin is still compatible. This is certainly a reasonable view, and many strong Christians and theological giants such as C. S. Lewis have held to that position.

I think the main thing we see, whether we believe in theistic evolution or a creation account of humans, is that humankind is unique. We see from the Scripture text that humans were created in the "image of God," which implies a differentiation from the animal kingdom. Although human beings demonstrate a much superior mental capability and an affective or emotional component, the primary differentiation, I believe, is spiritual. As humans, we have the ability to study the universe, observe its makeup, and ponder its beginning—but also to know and understand God. Genesis 2:7 says the man became a living "soul," which I think implies a deeper spiritual quality that is different from the qualities of the animal kingdom. With this spiritual component, I believe humankind was given the spiritual capacity to relate to and know God. I think this means that, as spirit beings, we can hear and receive God's word. We can enter into relationship with God. We can pray and sense God's Spirit and see the tangible results of his hand in the world, as we did with *Apollo 13*. No other creature can do that.

In conclusion, it is fascinating to study the parallel creation theme—where days 1–3 are aligned in parallel to days 4–6—and compare it with the cosmological and geological history of what we know about the development of the universe; there is a broad degree of association and agreement between the two perspectives.[14] What we see from this perspective is a theological picture of God's provision and love—where there was a need (a void), God's love and creative energy filled that need. Then he created humankind to relate to him and worship him. The creation account is depicted in seven days, where the seventh day, the Sabbath Day in Jewish chronology, is a day to worship God, which might be viewed as the ultimate purpose of creation. Therefore, what we find in this ancient text on origins is an account consistent with modern scientific understanding. But beyond that, it is a theological statement on God's character and our relationship to God. As Weaver notes, it is interesting to point out and observe how an person writing some 2,500 to 3,000 years ago was able to present an outline order of creation consistent with what has been established scientifically only in the last 200 years.[15]

Also, as indicated above, I think being created in God's likeness is an awesome truth, as we realize that the spiritual potential of humankind is immense. As spirit beings, we can hear God's word and ride it to untold spiritual heights. We can enter into that "thin-space" of spiritual connectivity and intersect with the divine. (I will discuss this more in the next chapter.) The text says we were made in the image of God (God's likeness), which means, as Scripture says elsewhere, that we can become "children of God." As children of God or spirit beings, I believe we can sense God's Spirit and see and experience the total Godhead: God the Father, Christ the Son, and God the Holy Spirit. And, as children of God, we are created in a sense to bear his image and rule over all creation. I am reminded of the verses from Psalm 8 that reflect on the uniqueness of humanity:

When I consider your heavens, the work of your fingers,
the moon and stars which you have set in place,
what is man that you are mindful of him,
the son of man that you care for him?
You have made him a little lower than the heavenly beings
and crowned him with glory and honor.
You have made him ruler of the works of your hands;
You put everything under his feet. (vv. 3-5)

Even though humankind was the crowing apex of God's creation, because of the free will component necessary for love, humans chose wrongfully and fell into sin, which broke the relationship with God. That resulted in a separated condition within us that was empty—unfulfilled without God. So, to restore and fulfill that relationship, God was gracious and provided a means of restoration through Christ the Son. Long ago, French physicist and mathematician Blaise Pascal said, "There is a God-shaped vacuum in the heart of each man which cannot be satisfied by any created thing but only by God the Creator, made known through Jesus Christ."[16] So again God filled the void—this time the void of brokenness, and this time with the incarnation, life, death, and resurrection of the Son. Through seeing (experiencing) the Son, we have a new origin: the rebirth or spiritual regeneration of humankind. That is the message of Christianity.

From a theological perspective, then, this ancient text on origins not only delineates an accounting of the beginning of the universe and humankind but also presents a set of theological truths. We can read about the origin of the universe and also the origin of the soul, the origin of sin, and the origin of humans with the capacity to know and worship God. As I personally reflect on these truths, I am consistently awed by an omnipotent God who loves to create life in all its forms and to give us the capability to know and be known, to love and be loved. In the next chapter, I will discuss more fully how the intersection of faith and science can reveal the truths of God's character.

Notes

1. John David Weaver, *In the Beginning God* (Oxford UK: Regents Park College in association with Smyth & Helwys Publishing, Inc. Macon GA, 1994) 106.

2. Ibid., 115.

3. David Atkinson, *The Message of Genesis 1-11*, The Bible Speaks Today (Leicester, England: IVP, 1990) 17.

4. Edward J. Young, *Studies in Genesis One* (Phillipsburg NJ: Presbyterian & Reformed Publishing, 1964) 82.

5. Weaver, *In the Beginning God*, 101.

6. Kent Hughes, *Genesis: Beginning & Blessing* (Wheaton IL: Good News Publishing, 2010) 24–25.

7. P. J. Wiseman, *Clues to Creation in Genesis* (London: Marshall, Morgan, & Scott, 1977) 118.

8. Hughes, *Genesis*, 27.

9. Ibid., 24–25.

10. Weaver, *In the Beginning God*, 113.

11. Ibid., 113.

12. Tim Keller, "Creation, Evolution, and Christian Laypeople, Part 3," 9 March 2012, biologos.org/blogs/archive/creation-evolution-and-christian-laypeople-part-3.

13. Keller, Tim, "Creation, Evolution, and Christian Laypeople, Part 4," 16 March 2012, biologos.org/blogs/archive/creation-evolution-and-christian-laypeople-part-4.

14. Weaver, *In the Beginning God*, 111.

15. Ibid., 114.

16. Quoted in Hughes, *Genesis*, 39.

Chapter 7

The Intersection of Faith and Science

In the "thin-space" between physical and spiritual realities, my spirit touched his.

I agree with noted physicist and priest John Polkinghorne, who says that there must be no compartmentalization between faith and science; both are held together by the Creator, who is the single foundation for all that is.[1] I believe there is a realness about human life that includes inspiration and spirituality as well as physical observation and measurement. While it is true that spiritual entities are invisible to the human eye, they are very real, indeed, and provide traces in the physical world, as I've delineated in previous chapters. As I mentioned in chapter 4, the spiritual world is a realm impossible to explore with the tools and language of science; it must be examined with the heart, the mind, and the soul. Faith is a spiritual reality, and spiritual realities lie beyond the range of our ordinary perceptions. Faith is a different dimension, a different sense or reality not perceived with our natural senses. In spite of this, however, I agree with Polkinghorne, who says that the Christian experience is one of the strongest indicators of the claim that religion (faith) is in touch with reality.[2]

In this chapter, I want to examine how faith and science intersect and relate to each other. How do they help each other? How do they witness to each other? They seem to crash into each other at times, with a lot of heat and noise at some points—perhaps not unlike the Big Bang itself—and yet at other times they seem to lift each other up and complement each other. Perhaps we find the "thin-space" of both realities at the point of this intersection, and perhaps we meet the Creator of the cosmos there.

Traditionally, science has primarily asked questions about "how." Faith has asked questions about "why." In a curious way, however, science now seems to be asking questions pointing to something beyond itself. Modern cosmologists are asking questions about the beginning and the end of the universe, about the place of humanity itself, and about the reasons for the apparent design of the universe. Theology seeks to make sense of the whole universe and aims to answer the questions that science is posing. Theology, for example, hears the questions raised by the fine-tuning of the universe and Brian Carter's anthropic principle (the improbability of so many constants taking on the values necessary for a stable universe that sustains complex life forms) and seeks to understand what it might mean to see the guiding hand of God within them.[3] For theologians, God is at the center of their study, and information about God comes through Scripture, revelation, and experience. For many scientists, humankind is at the center, and information comes through observation, measurement, and analysis, where the scientist is the analyzer or interpreter.

Many scientists, like Stephen Hawking, hope to find a grand unifying Theory of Everything that would explain how all laws work and how the Big Bang happened. Hawking ends his book, *A Brief History of Time*, with the hope of finding a unified theory that would combine quantum physics, general relativity, and gravity. If we could find such a unified theory, we would, he claims, be able to discern why we and the universe exist.[4] On the other hand, I believe that theology or faith tries to bring together the issues that affect both science and faith itself. As I have mentioned earlier, however, we should realize

THE INTERSECTION OF FAITH AND SCIENCE 85

that both faith and science are searching for truth, and the two sides should collaborate to see how we could support each other.

Another view about science and faith suggests that there is a profound connection between the mind of humankind and the work of God. It is a remarkable thing that humans are able to do science in the first place—that we can, to some degree, "figure out" the cosmos. It is amazing that humans possess the cognitive ability to reason and engineer designs that probe the universe. A switch is thrown, and a rocket ignites. Spaceships land on the Moon and return to Earth safely. Some scientists and engineers ask questions like, "Why should the laws of nature be comprehensible and accessible to humans? Are these cognitive abilities simply coincidence with no deeper meaning?" Other scientists and theologians suspect, however, that the interconnectivity of the intellectual ability of humankind and the longing or drive for truth reflects something more profound. The fact that we have a mind (an intellect) to discover and understand the universe suggests the possibility of a divine Creator who has given us a mind with the ability to understand the cosmos and also to understand and relate to its Creator. The ontological argument for God's existence is the classical Christian argument that contends that the very concept of God logically and necessarily demands existence based on our ability to reason and think.

Wolfhart Pannenberg has recognized that many scientists in a variety of fields are facing questions, often of a moral nature, that they do not have the resources to deal with. He believes there should be discussion between organized religion and the scientific community and urges the need for integration of faith and science:

> If the God of the Bible is the creator of the universe, then it is not possible to understand fully, or even appropriately, the process of nature without reference to that God. If, on the contrary, nature can be appropriately understood without reference to the God of the Bible, then that God cannot be the creator of the universe, and consequently he could not be truly God and could not be trusted as the source of moral teaching either.[5]

In the previous chapter, I discussed some apparent conflicts between science and faith, but beyond that, I hope we can see the positive influence that each can have on the other. We should avoid the dualism that separates science and religious faith and recognize that our total comprehension and apprehension of the real world is both spiritual and physical. Just as science shows us there are realities we cannot see with the naked eye—such as electron flow and electromagnetic radiation, which we pack with gigabytes of information for computer and TV usage—so there are spiritual realities we cannot see visually, such as spiritual rebirth and prayer, and these are just as useful and helpful for one's quality of life. Unfortunately, there has been a division between science and faith, heightened by the strong influence of the scientific world on individual beliefs and values. I believe, however, that God intended that the spirit life bear the greatest influence and bring positive change to our values, actions, and way of life.

For my comparison of science and faith in this chapter, I want to mention again the words of Einstein: "Religion without science is blind, and science without religion is lame." As I stated earlier, I think he meant that religion can't see far without help, and science is an important window that gives us vision into the spiritual world. The second part of his statement insists that science without religion (faith) is "lame"—or, I would say, without spiritual life, which is in reality the truest life. I again agree with Polkinghorne, who further extrapolated Einstein's statement by saying, "Religion without science is confined; it fails to be completely open to reality. . . . Science without religion is incomplete; it fails to attain the deepest possible meaning."[6] I would add that not only does science fail to understand the deepest meaning but also, without faith, it lacks connection with real life. I believe God desires for humankind a deeper level of experience, connecting with all the color and fullness of life.

So first, let us examine how religion without science is "confined," or as Einstein would say, "blind." As I expressed in chapter 5, science opens a tremendous window into the spiritual world. Of all the disciplines, science seems to be bursting forth with new and insightful data that "boggles the mind" and presents a universe of unbelievable

THE INTERSECTION OF FAITH AND SCIENCE

complexity and intricate design. Everywhere we look—whether into the deepest recesses of space or the minutia of the microscope—the intricacy, precision, and complexity of the universe staggers us with the enormity of details and vastness of information. Contemporary astronomy and astrophysics, as well as nuclear and particle physics, are hurling new knowledge at us at breathtaking speed. Even as I write this book, the proof of gravitational wave theory is breaking onto the scene. As a Christian, I am encouraged by the discoveries of modern science that uncover a universe whose initial conditions were so finely tuned as to produce human life, conscious awareness, and the ability to contemplate the universe of which we are a part. I believe that since God is the ultimate designer and creator of the universe, "all truth is God's truth," and we have nothing to fear with new scientific discovery. However, the recognition of something like intelligent design is only the beginning to further steps of belief in a supreme being. We are challenged to go beyond these beliefs to understand the true character of God and the spiritual truths illustrated by the design of the universe.

For the Christian theologian, these factors in contemporary science are not only suggestive of the existence of God but also give insight and reflect on the nature and character of God. The overwhelming vastness and magnificent design of the universe, as I discussed in chapter 5, reflect an omniscient and omnipotent God. The dependability of the laws of the universe can be seen as signs of God's faithfulness and dependability. The beauty and intricate design of the numerous life forms of this world unveil a God who loves beauty and life in all its forms. I have previously noted that at the subatomic level and in some subsystems, there is an apparent chaotic behavior that would appear to move us away from a mechanistic, deterministic universe, in which God stands aloof on the outside uninvolved. It appears that a God allowing this chaotic type of behavior would have to allow free will yet be involved in the universe at all levels.

Reflection on this type of universe and on life forms—with characteristics such as free will and a desire to live—prompts us to think of a personal God who values life and intercedes to repair and redeem. This certainly rings true with what we find in Holy Scripture depicting God's character, particularly in passages such as Luke 15, where Jesus tells the parable of a father greatly rejoicing over a son who is lost and then is found. This, along with many other passages, reflects a God who places great value on human life. I see this valuing of human life coming from the heart of a good and loving God who has tremendous motivation and desire to redeem and relate to humankind.

The study of the cosmos and nuclear physics also reveals another fundamental spiritual truth or life principle that I have come to understand and appreciate. That is, for new life or energy (and mass) to be generated, an element or seed of life must die or be changed. Take for instance the formation of stars and nuclear fusion, which illustrate this principle. Stars are formed as a result of an outside disturbing force that moves through vast clouds of interstellar dust and gas. Particles collide and form a clump that attracts more and more mass. The clump grows into a dense body called a protostar. When the protostar gets hot enough, its hydrogen atoms begin to fuse. And when the hydrogen atoms fuse, they combine (thus losing their old identity) and produce helium (a new element is born) and an outflow of energy. This is happening all the time in the nuclear fusion of stars; new elements and tremendous energy are released even as the old stars die. Interestingly, the energy released from our own star is needed to sustain life on our planet.

Perhaps a more familiar illustration of this principle is revealed in the field of biology and shown by Christ himself. A simple seed containing the germ of life must be buried and die, in a sense, to produce a new plant. This illustrates beautifully the underlying spiritual truth that God, in his great love for humankind, entered into the humanity he created, made himself known as the Son, and gave himself up in death that he might reconcile (reunite) humanity. It is the great law of the universe. Springing forth out of the Son's death is the generation and capability for new life in us as humans.

Another example of science helping religion is that science has made theologians look more closely at their interpretation of Scripture. Science is sort of a theological corrective to a strictly literal interpretation of Scripture. In the sixteenth century, Copernicus proposed that the Sun and not the Earth was the center of the solar system. Galileo supported this theory but ran into dire conflict with the church. Others came along, like Kepler, who established that the planes of all planetary orbits pass through the Sun—and the church was forced to rethink its position. Then, when Darwin came along in the nineteenth century with his theory of evolution, biblical scholars and the church were challenged again to rethink their position on creation. Of course, this debate still goes on to this day, with credible scholars on both sides. This sort of discovery and debate forces Christians to take an honest and critical look at the genre, context, and word meanings of Scripture.

In the seventeenth century, Archbishop Ussher calculated the age of the Earth up to the birth of Christ to be around 4,000 years using biblical genealogies. Prior to the nineteenth century, most people took the age of the Earth to be around 6,000 years, based on Ussher and other biblical chronologists. In the early nineteenth century, though, geologists began postulating an older Earth somewhere around a million years old. Then, with the development of radiometric dating in the early twentieth century, the age of the Earth was calculated at 4.5 billion years using data from several sources. The radiometric calculation of the Earth's age is based on the half-life decay of three primary radioactive elements that transform into different elements. Measurements from all three of these elements have yielded amazingly similar results pointing to the age of the Earth now accepted by most scientists as 4.5 billion years. Also, rocks from the Moon and several meteorites have now been dated and yield similar results. Young Earth creationists still hold to an Earth age of around 6,000–8,000 years based on other data that I noted in chapter 4. But, considering more recent biblical studies, it is now clear from the rest of the Bible that the genealogies used for earlier dating of the Earth were telescoped (that is, some names were left out for the sake of brevity), which is common in biblical genealogies but rare in modern genealogies. By cross-referencing the biblical genealogies with other events dated in the Bible, one can find instances where numerous genealogies were telescoped, resulting in the exclusion of several generations of individuals. Similarly, the key genealogical terms (such as "son" and "father") have much broader meanings in Hebrew than their corresponding English words. The Hebrew word translated "son," for example, can also have the meaning of "grandson," "great-grandson," or "descendant." Likewise, the Hebrew word translated "father" can mean "grandfather," "great-grandfather," "ancestor," etc. Having a proper understanding of biblical genealogies and languages is a prerequisite for attempting to address the Genesis genealogies and historical time lines.

We are therefore benefitted by science, which drives us back to Scripture to see what God is really trying to tell us. In my case, discoveries in the field of science have made me study Scripture more critically and even turned up interesting and more profound truths than I had understood before. Other verses come into play, and we begin to see a new characteristic of God we hadn't thought of (for example, his longsuffering and patience with humanity). Sometimes we are so steeped in the upbringing and preconditioning of our views that we cannot see a different view, or at least find it hard to do so. It is that way with many things in life. We need to honestly check our hearts for the motivation and reason for our beliefs.

On the other side of Einstein's philosophical equation (science without religion), religion helps science—or more accurately, it helps our psychological self and our scientific mindset to answer some of the deeper questions that science and humanity are asking. I believe that theology and the answers found in the Christian faith have a great deal to offer the scientific community and humanity in general. We live in a world where there is a longing and a quest for ultimate meaning and purpose. There is unrest and anxiety over human finitude, evil, suffering, and death. Through "religion," we come to realize that the Christian faith provides answers to these deepest needs and gives meaning to life. As mentioned earlier, a study of the Bible shows that the grand purpose of the universe is to help us (humanity) come to know and worship God. I believe that since God has limited himself and given humankind a free will, evil is the product of freedom misused, and suffering results from bad choices and the struggle of conflicting goals. So having a faith component to our worldview helps us make more sense of the natural world.

With respect to suffering caused by natural disasters, I believe the Earth was created and developed with a set of laws and mechanisms in place—but, with the spiritual "fall" of humanity, God has limited himself within nature to allow some randomness and chaotic behavior that produce storms and fractures in the Earth's crust. The Earth and creation are slowly deteriorating. Even Scripture speaks to this when it says, "For creation was subjected to frustration, not by its own choice, but by the will of the one who subjected it, in hope that the creation itself will be liberated from its bondage to decay. . . . We know that the whole creation has been groaning as in pains of childbirth right up to the present time" (Rom 8:20-22). God, however, seeks to redeem and restore humanity and creation by working with us. As human beings, we should also recognize that we are in a sense God's representatives on Earth, called to understand the creation and work with him to care for and rule over (master) the Earth. German theologian Jürgen Moltmann describes our role on Earth like this:

> As God's image and appearance on earth, human beings are involved in three fundamental relationships: they rule over other earthly creatures as God's representatives and in his name; they are God's counterpart on earth, the counterpart to whom he wants to talk; and they are the appearance of God's splendor, and his glory on earth.[7]

Human beings are given the freedom and purpose to work with God to help humanity improve our planet's ecological well-being. Awareness of the ecological interdependence of the Earth and humankind is recognized as critical and alerts us to an important role of people. Science and the moral component of faith must then work together in a combined dynamic to improve and extend life on planet Earth.

The world of science is an interesting and compelling discipline. It challenges the intellect and the soul and can be quite rewarding as new discoveries and truths are unveiled. However, we may search and search, and even discover amazing truths about the universe, yet still come up "flat" without connecting to God. For God has placed within us an eternal spirit that longs to be whole, longs to be redeemed, longs to connect and even worship. Science can provide a sense of joy and satisfaction in uncovering indescribable truths, but there is a sense of yearning within us to understand some greater truth. As Francis Collins suggests, it is an inkling of what lies beyond, a signpost placed deep within the human spirit pointing to something much greater than ourselves.[8]

While at NASA, I found a certain amount of satisfaction and discovery in my own pursuit of engineering and scientific studies, yet I was often left with that inner question of the soul: "Is this all there is?" During the Skylab program of the early seventies (which was a forerunner of the International Space Station), we collected mounds of data in many fields of scientific research. There were also numerous delicately designed instruments that we had the satisfaction and frustration of dealing with. We worked with various Principal Investigators who did creative research in stellar observation, solar studies, galactic mapping, Earth resources, and various other science technologies. Although many of their findings were remarkable and drew numerous interesting conclusions, in many cases their results only left them in a quandary, with many more unanswered questions. It seems that in many disciplines, when we come to understand a certain behavior or phenomena, it only unveils a complexity that reveals a further mystery.

Science can probe the vastness of space, the depths of the oceans, and the intricacies of the microscopic world; it can illuminate mysteries that have been covered for hundreds of years and engineer applications to make our life easier. Yet there are deeper mysteries and truths that only faith can unlock, connecting with our heart and soul for a full and abundant life. Our minds and souls are still troubled, and there is often a longing that still prevails. As Pascal said we have a "God-shaped vacuum" deep within our hearts and minds that is meant to be filled. Science can stir the mind, but only God can satisfy the soul.

In our modern materialistic world, it is easy to lose sight of that sense of longing. Annie Dillard speaks about the growing void in her collection of essays, *Teaching a Stone to Talk*, sharing the following:

Now we are no longer primitive. Now the whole world seems not holy. . . . We as a people have moved from pantheism to pan-atheism . . . . We doused the burning bush and cannot rekindle it. We are lighting matches in vain under every green tree. Did the wind used to cry and the hills shout forth praise? What have we been doing all these centuries but trying to call God back to the mountain, or, failing that, raise a peep out of anything that isn't us? What is the difference between a cathedral and a physics lab? Are they not both saying: Hello?[9]

If we listen closely, however, science *and* faith are showing us truths and values that relate to the deepest longings and needs of our being.

There is a limit, though, to how far science can take us in our understanding of the deeper questions and yearnings of life. I would agree with and appreciate the assessment of former NASA astrophysicist Robert Jastrow, who stated,

For the scientist who has lived by his faith in the power of reason, the story ends like a bad dream. He has scaled the mountains of ignorance; he is about to conquer the highest peak; and as he pulls himself over the final rock, he is greeted by a band of theologians who have been sitting there for centuries.[10]

In conclusion, I believe that the Bible and science show us much about the character and nature of God. First of all, I agree with John Weaver in believing that science clearly shows us something of the supremacy and transcendence of God.[11] I believe the evidence is brilliantly displayed in the universe that God is an all-powerful, omniscient, and preeminent being whose rational mind is both behind and before a created universe. We have seen that science has gradually made discoveries that suggest a God who is transcendent in bringing the universe into existence. This transcendent view collaborates well with the biblical disclosure of God from several Bible passages:

Genesis 1:1: "In the beginning God created the heavens and the earth."

Job 9:8-9: "He alone stretches out the heavens . . . . He is the maker of the Bear and Orion, Pleiades and the constellations."

Job 26:7: "He spreads out the northern skies over empty space; he suspends the earth over nothing."

Isaiah 40:22, 28: "He sits enthroned above the circle [sphere] of the earth. . . . He stretches out the heavens like a canopy . . . . Do you not know? Have you not heard? The LORD is the everlasting God, the Creator of the ends of the earth."

Psalm 104:24-25: "How many are your works O LORD! In wisdom you made them all; the earth is full of your creatures. There is the sea, vast and spacious, teaming with creatures beyond number—living things both large and small."

These verses and others describe the transcendent nature of a Creator God who has the power and wisdom to create life in all its forms; and science has given us a window to more fully appreciate the intricacies and magnificence of their design.

I also believe that science also shows us the presence and immanence of God—his involvement and care for his creation. I don't believe in a Newtonian or deistic view of God where God is not involved in our universe. To the contrary, I believe God's involvement is shown through the physical laws and resources that maintain and regenerate our planet. Science is helping us understand the magnitude, majesty, and purpose that are found in an evolving universe, which therefore helps us understand more about the care of God for his creation.[12] Through the resiliency of humanity and the re-creation of the Earth, based on the nature of the Earth and its physical laws, science demonstrates God's involvement to care for humanity.

The Bible clearly presents this immanent view through the revelation of God's word in the Bible in passages like these:

THE INTERSECTION OF FAITH AND SCIENCE   95

Job 36:26-28: "How great is God—[he is] beyond our understanding. He draws up the drops of water which distill as rain to the
streams; the clouds pour down their moisture and abundant showers
fall on mankind."

Psalm 104:14-15: "He makes grass grow for the cattle, and plants
for man to cultivate—bringing forth food from the earth; wine that
gladdens the heart of man, oil to make his face shine, and bread that
sustains his heart."

Psalm 107:35: "He turned the desert into pools of water and the
parched ground into flowing springs."

Isaiah 40:11, 28-31: "He tends his flock like a shepherd; he gathers
the lambs in his arms and carries them close to his heart; he gently
leads those that have young. . . . He will not grow tired or weary, and
his understanding no one can fathom. He gives strength to the weary
and increases the power of the weak. Even the youths grow tired and
weary, and young men stumble and fall; but those who hope in the
LORD will renew their strength. They will soar on wings like eagles;
they will run and not be weary, they will walk and not faint."

Throughout the Bible, we see this immanent view of a God who is
intimately involved with humankind—creating, shaping, nurturing,
and redeeming his creation.

I wanted to add a little suffix to this chapter as a testimony to a
transcendent God who is also personal. It was a small thing, really,
yet inspirational and encouraging to me of the reality of a personal
God who affirms his children. During the day that I was wrapping
up this chapter and searching for appropriate Scriptures to use as a
reference for the ideas I was discussing, I ran across the Scripture
above (Isa 40:28-29) that I had probably heard a few times in my
life. It seemed to speak to me anew as I contemplated the awesomeness of a God who is not only the Creator but who also cares and
strengthens us in the time of our need. Then, lo and behold, some six
hours later when I went to choir practice that evening, as I normally

do on a Wednesday night, our music director had picked out a song to practice ("Our God Is God" by Paul Williams/Joseph Martin) that I had never heard in my fifty-plus years of church life but that was based on the very passage I had studied earlier in the day and echoed those words in my mind. Coincidence? I think not. To me, it was miraculous; God was once again orchestrating events. As I sang the words from the song—"Have you not heard, do you not know? Who formed the stars, called them by name? Who calms the storm, sends gentle rain . . . Our God is God"[13]—my heart was stirred to realize what an awesome God we have. Once again, in that "thin-space" between the physical and spiritual realities of the cosmos, my spirit touched God's Spirit—or perhaps I should say God's Spirit touched my spirit—and I was awed at the hand of a transcendent God who reached down and touched my soul.

Notes

1. John C. Polkinghorne, *Science and Creation* (London, SPCK, 1988) 69.

2. John C. Polkinghorne, *Science & Theology: An Introduction* (Minneapolis: Fortress Press, 1998) 29.

3. John David Weaver, *In the Beginning God* (Oxford UK: Regents Park College in association with Smyth & Helwys Publishing, Inc., Macon GA, 1994) 11.

4. Stephen W. Hawking, *A Brief History of Time* (New York: Bantam Books, 1998) 175.

5. Weaver, *In the Beginning God*, 156.

6. Polkinghorne, *Science and Creation*, 97.

7. Jürgen Moltmann, *God in Creation, An Ecological Doctrine of Creation*, The Gifford Lectures 1984-1985, trans. M. Kohl (London: SCM, 1985) 57.

8. Francis S. Collins, *The Language of God* (New York: Free Press, 2006) 37.

9. Annie Dillard, *Teaching a Stone to Talk* (New York: Harper Perennial, 1992) 87.

10. Robert Jastrow, *God and the Astronomers* (New York: W. W. Norton & Company, 1992) 107.

11. Weaver, *In the Beginning God*, 175.

12. Ibid.

13. J. Paul Williams and Joseph Martin, "Our God Is God" (Nashville TN: Shawnee Press, 2006) 3, 4.

Chapter 8

Seeing the Son, Knowing the Father

Journey of Discovery

Coming to know God as Father has been a journey of discovery for me that is still incomplete—it is, in fact, a journey of a lifetime. As a young boy of around eight years old, I loved baseball and played at school and with a neighborhood boy across the street. We would play catch almost every day. There was a neighborhood Baptist church just a few blocks from our house, and as it turned out, the pastor lived only a few houses beyond ours, and he would often walk by our house on the way to church. He frequently stopped and played ball with us, as he enjoyed baseball himself. He invited our family to visit the church, and my mom started attending and dragged me and my brother and sister along as well. Although I wasn't a particularly bad kid, I had smoked a grapevine once and was a little mischievous, as my best friend and I were good at playing tricks on some of the other school and church kids. The pastor had to call us into the church office several times for such offenses as stealing cookies and squirting other kids with water guns during Vacation Bible School.

By the age of twelve, I had heard a number of Bible stories about the love of God and the death, burial, and resurrection of Christ for our sins. I realized that I, too, had a sinful heart and that something was missing in my life, and I wanted the abundant life that Jesus talked about in the Bible. So I believed, accepted Christ in simple childlike faith, and was baptized at the Sagamore Hill Baptist Church in Fort Worth, Texas. It was through Christ that I experienced a spiritual birth at that young age and began my spiritual journey to know and experience the Father. The concept of "Father" may be difficult for those who have a bad experience with their earthly father, but the model of God as Father was taught by Christ, as he taught his disciples to address God as "Father." Even though I have struggled many times, had doubts, and gone through various renewals of my faith, I believe that my early faith experience as a twelve-year-old boy was genuine for me and has stuck with me all my life.

As I think about my personal faith journey and the numerous ways God reveals himself to us, my mind turns to the ultimate purpose of creation and God's interaction with humanity in the world. I have come to realize that the world is not just a physical place in which we live and work and care for our planet; it is a place into which God enters and re-creates, relates to people, and is revealed. The Bible indicates that God's plan and purpose in creation is more of a relational nature. David Atkinson says, "God's relationship with the world is one of dynamic and creative interaction."[1] From the beginning, it has been evident that God has been and is continually working to re-create us, renew us, and draw us to himself. The incarnation of Christ supremely points to God's dynamic and intimate relationship with the world. As the familiar passage in the Gospel of John states, "For God so loved the world that he gave his one and only Son, that whoever believes in him shall not perish but have eternal life. For God did not send his Son into the world to condemn the world, but to save the world through him" (John 3:16-17).

As I mentioned earlier, although cosmology helps us understand something of the majesty, magnitude, and omnipotence of God, it is not the same as *knowing* God. The revelation of God through cosmology reaches its limit when it brings us to uncover what we may think of as an Awesome Designer. This point of view brings us only to see a Newtonian type of God. For Isaac Newton, God was the creator and repairer of the universe and kept the planets from

SEEING THE SON, KNOWING THE FATHER

crashing into each other. Newton was a deeply religious man who thought of the universe as the rational design of God, but his scientific view kept God outside the universe and did not allow for the incarnation of God in Christ Jesus.[2]

Although God's revelation to us through the glory and majesty of the cosmos is an enlightening first step for many, the God and Father of our Lord Jesus Christ must be sought through other means, such as prayer, Bible study, and worship. I believe it is important to come to know and relate to God because that was his ultimate purpose in creation. If we don't know the Father well, we develop a skewed understanding of God that misshapes our worldview and prevents us from enjoying life to the fullest. God's goal for us as individuals is that we might relate to him and experience an abundant life. Again, in the Gospel of John we read, "I have come that you might have life, and that you might have it more abundantly" (John 10:10).

In the New Testament, Jesus tells a story that gives us some insight about the importance of knowing and relating to the Father. It is found in Matthew 25 and is actually a parable about stewardship and being faithful with what we have been given. It goes something like this: A wealthy landowner was going on a journey, and he gave some of his servants various sums of money to invest while he was gone. To one he gave five talents, to another two, and to another one, each according to his own abilities. The servant who had been given the five talents went and put the money to work and gained five more talents, and the one who had been given two did likewise. However, the servant who had been given one talent dug a hole and hid it in the ground. After a long time the master returned and called his servants in for an accounting of the money they had been entrusted with. The first servant gladly presented the result that he had gained five talents more, and the second servant did likewise. The master blessed them and invited them to share in the master's happiness. The third servant had nothing to show for his talent and said to the master, "I *knew* that you were a hard man, trying to harvest where you have not sown." To which the master replied, "You lazy servant. So you *knew* I harvested where I had not sown. You should have invested my money with a banker." The lazy servant only thought he knew the master. The servant's talent was taken away and he was banished outside the kingdom.

The primary teaching of this parable is to be a faithful steward of the resources and talents we have been entrusted with, but a secondary teaching revolves around the importance of "knowing" the master. The lazy servant thought he knew the master, but he really didn't. He thought his master was a hard man, but in reality the master was gracious. He thought his master would harvest where he had not sown, but again by implication the servant didn't truly know the master. The servant not only lost his relationship with the master but was also banned from the kingdom. In today's culture, I believe that in the same way many people have a misshapen view of God and the Christian faith; they have never taken the time to examine Christianity and understand its truths.

Now that I have underscored the importance of relating to God and shared something of the revelation of God through cosmology and through "God-like" events in our lives, I come to the ultimate question: How do we cross over from the physical into that "thin-space" of the spiritual realm in order to experience God? How do we come to know and relate to God in a personal way? Do we pursue God, or does God pursue us?

First of all, Jesus' teachings in the New Testament make it clear that he is the door; he is the way of finding true relationship with the Father. Scriptures such as John 10:7, 9 ("I tell you the truth, I am the door for the sheep . . . whoever enters through me will be saved") and John 14:6 ("I am the way and the truth and the life; no one comes to the Father except through me") are prime examples. As I have emphasized already, God has been revealing himself throughout history through the marvelous message of the cosmos, through numerous prophets (dreams, visions, audible and inaudible hearing of God's voice), through miracles, through Scripture, and finally by making himself known through the incarnation of Christ. Although Christ is no longer with us physically, we have all this evidence that there is something going on in the spiritual realm. It's true that crossing over into the spiritual dimension that is not seen with our physical eyes takes a "leap of faith." Faith is the key that opens the door or ushers us into the "thin-space" of spiritual reality. But I believe our faith is not a "blind faith" or a "leap" into nothingness.

What is faith? Faith is defined as belief with strong conviction; a firm belief in something for which there may be little or no tangible proof; complete trust, confidence, reliance, or devotion. In the New Testament in Hebrews 11:1, the writer says, "Faith is being sure of what we hope for and certain of what we do not see." The Greek word for "being sure," *hypostasis,* means "substance" or "confidence." It is the confidence we have that God is God. Perhaps we can better understand faith when we see what faith is not. Faith is not a feeling, a hunch, or even intellectual assent; it is the solid certainty of belief based on our experiences—what we see in the natural world, in other's lives, in Scripture, and in how God has intervened in our own lives.

In a sense, faith therefore becomes a transformer that enables spiritual "transformation." In an electrical circuit, a transformer can take an extremely high voltage and convert it to a low voltage that can be used to operate our laptops. Likewise, faith becomes a spiritual transformer by which the extremely high power of the divine is made spiritually available to our hearts and souls. Faith is the spiritual converter or alteration by which we are enabled to see the invisible, just as our eyes behold the physical world around us. Faith is not a one-time event or static. It is a lifestyle continuum. In theological studies there are stages of faith, from a simple child-like faith to a more mature or conjunctive faith—defined by James Fowler as a faith in which one faces up to the paradoxes and heartaches of life and begins to develop a more mature and universal concept of faith.[3] Faith opens the door by which we are spiritually "born," but this is only the beginning.

Our spiritual pilgrimage or relationship with God must be continually nurtured, or we become dry and grow stale. We sense a loss of connectivity with God—our prayers go no higher than the ceiling. As to the question of whether God pursues us or we pursue God, I think it is both. As English poet Francis Thompson expresses in his famous poem, *The Hound of Heaven,* God continually pursues us, seeking us like a lost child; and as J. F. X. O'Conor's commentary elaborates,

> As the hound follows the hare, never ceasing in its running, ever drawing nearer in the chase, with unhurrying and unperturbed pace, so does God follow the fleeing soul by His Divine grace; and though in sin or in human love, away from God it seeks to hide itself, Divine grace follows after, unwearyingly follows ever after, till the soul feels its pressure forcing it to turn to Him alone in that never ending pursuit.[4]

I too have felt God pursuing me my whole life—guiding me, nudging me, prompting me, orchestrating events to demonstrate his handiwork. But then, on the other hand, I think we also pursue God, seeking him and longing to fill the void or chasm that separates us.

There are several ways of connecting and nurturing our relationship with God, and I turn now to summarizing some of these. First and foremost is prayer. Prayer is the two-way communion we have with the Father. We have the sense that we can communicate with the Great God of the universe. There are several example prayers in Scripture, probably the most notable being what is commonly called the "Lord's Prayer" or the "Model Prayer" (Matt 6:9-13), which was prayed by the Lord in response to a question his disciples asked about how to pray. It contains the basic elements of prayer: adoration ("Our Father in heaven, hallowed be your name"), confession ("forgive us our debts"), trust and hope ("your kingdom come, your will be done"), petition ("give us this day our daily bread"), and protection from evil ("lead us not into temptation, and deliver us from evil"). Other prayers and instructions from Jesus emphasize God's great goodness and desire to give us good gifts, such as Matthew 7:7-11: "If a son asks [his father] for bread, will [he] give him a stone, or if he asks for a fish, will [he] give him a snake? If you being evil know how to give good gifts to your children, how much more will your Father in heaven give good gifts to those ask him?" We ask for specific things and see specific results—a sickness cured, protection from harmful events and circumstances, deliverance of three astronauts from impending disaster. From time immemorial,

SEEING THE SON, KNOWING THE FATHER

prayer has provided comfort and protection in times of trial, direction and guidance in times of struggle, and motivation to act in times of insurmountable challenges. As I have related earlier in this book, I am convinced that it was the prayers of my Christian cohort and me, along with thousands of others, that got us through the challenges of the *Apollo 13* crisis.

A few years ago my wife and I, along with my mother- and father-in-law, were returning from a short-term mission trip to the Amazon region of Venezuela. We were departing from a small town in the Amazon to return to Caracas via a VIASA (Venezuelan airline) turboprop airplane. There was only one flight out over two or three days. A bad omen initially should have warned us. We waited several hours before we were allowed to board, and once on the plane we waited another hour on the tarmac while the crew had to obtain "clearance" from Caracas because of reported mechanical difficulties—supposedly hydraulic problems. As the plane cranked up for the preflight checkout, I noticed a puff of smoke on the right engine and the prop stopping and restarting. Nothing to worry about! We lifted off and, once airborne, chatted happily about the sights we had seen in the Amazon and the native Venezuelans who had come to know the Lord. The flight attendants ran through their standard safety instructions. We looked out the window and saw where the mighty Amazon River mingled with the Orinoco on the border of Colombia.

After an hour or two into the flight, without any explanation, we were suddenly startled by an announcement by the flight attendants that we were going to have to make an emergency landing. We didn't know if there was an emergency landing strip or whether they meant crash-landing in the Amazon jungle. The flight attendants didn't lend any confidence when they instructed us to bend over, put our heads between our knees, and grab the backs of our necks for the landing. All of these instructions were in Spanish, of course. I then saw the right engine stop (the same one I saw smoking late in the preflight). I looked at my wife, Shirley, and she looked at me, and we cringed at the thought of our children and family losing both their parents and grandparents in one fell swoop. It was one of those moments when you see your whole life pass before you. You talk about prayer—Shirley and I prayed! The plane dropped in altitude but continued to cruise.

Shortly afterward, the flight attendants, seemingly much relieved, announced that the pilot thought we could make it to Caracas, but that we had no brakes. That could be dicey, as the Caracas landing strip pretty much dropped off into the ocean at the end of the runway. We continued to pray, and the plane continued to cruise. We reached the Caracas airport and were told we were okay to land but still had no primary braking. The pilot said he would use emergency braking but that there was the possibility of fire. Below we could see numerous emergency vehicles standing by. We hit the runway, and, miracle of miracles, landed successfully—although sensing that we were not far from the end of the strip. We were immediately surrounded by an army of emergency crewmen dressed in silver fire suits, looking something like spacemen from a sci-fi movie. We were hurriedly escorted out of the plane and praised the Lord for a safe landing. Shirley vowed never to fly VIASA again!

We all know that God does not always answer with healing or deliverance—that is the great mystery of the divine—but in the very act of praying, we often sense a presence of his Spirit, and our hearts are drawn ever closer to his. We also must remember that prayer is a two-way street; we not only voice a prayer to the Holy One but also close our eyes and listen for the divine wind of the cosmos. It may not be an audible voice, but we sense his Spirit and experience events that seem to be miraculously orchestrated by God.

Another important way of connecting with God is through worship. One of the primary elements of worship is prayer, particularly in private worship. But I'm speaking here of the corporate worship exemplified by the New Testament Christians who continually assembled together to worship and fellowship. Something about the gathering of the church in corporate worship adds a sense of inspiration and closeness to God, as the church body worships together. One might ask, what is worship? To me, worship is characterized by the word "relationship." We relate to the Father. As I mentioned earlier in chapter 4, Jesus' exchange with the Samaritan woman as recorded in John 4 describes the essence of true worship as being in "Spirit and truth." I believe that means we experience true worship when our spirits resonate and relate with God's Spirit. Then we worship in truth when we hear truth revealed to us. God himself imparts guidance and wisdom, and our souls are lifted to sense the divine.

There are many components and expressions of worship—Scripture reading, singing, dancing, preaching, giving testimonies, baptism, Communion, giving, praying, and praise. Hopefully all of these put us in touch with the Father. As we praise the Lord, several things happen in our own spirits. We are drawn to God; we connect with God. As we realize and affirm God's greatness and righteousness, our own faith is strengthened. Someone has said that praise is the "spark plug" of faith. In other words, as we affirm and praise the Lord, the ignition of our praise results in greater trust and faith and moves us to action. Also, as we praise, God lifts our spirits of heaviness and gives us spirits of joy. As we praise, I believe that in some mysterious way the depths of our souls and hearts reach out, and we are made whole. Many Scriptures admonish us to praise, like this passage from Psalms:

> Praise the LORD. Praise the LORD from heavens; praise him from the heights above. Praise him, all his angels, praise all his heavenly hosts. Praise him sun and moon; praise him all you shining stars. Praise him, you highest heavens and you waters above the skies. Let them praise the name of the LORD, for he commanded and they were created. He set them in place for ever and ever; he gave a decree that will never pass away. Praise the LORD from the earth, you great sea creatures and all ocean depths . . . kings of the earth and all nations, you princes and rulers on earth, young men and maidens, old men and children. (Ps 148:1-7, 11-12)

Another positive way we connect with the Father and find nourishment for our souls is through Bible study. After some fifty years of study, I still believe that the Scriptures were divinely inspired and preserved to give us guidance and insight about God's character, instruction, and how to rightly relate with him and our fellow humans. Scholars and theologians can debate various means by which we received the Bible, but I believe it is still God's authentic word to us and for us. I believe this because I have seen the change in people's lives after exposure to the Scripture and its own testimony to itself. In several places, Scripture speaks about how it was "God-breathed," as its writers were moved by the Holy Spirit. In my own life, I believed this so strongly that after twenty-eight years I left my NASA career and pursued further education and training in theological and biblical studies.

Scripture is one of those connections with God where his words to us are more tangible than prayer—we often experience a more specific direction or communication from God. The Bible has specific things to say about specific things. When we need guidance, Scripture often provides insight. When we are depressed or sorrowful, Scripture can lift us up. When we rejoice, Scripture rejoices with us. When we need instruction and direction, Scripture can show us the way. I personally have experienced several situations in which I have been studying or listening to someone teaching Scripture, and the words and message of the passage jumped out and applied directly to the point of need in my life. Scripture also reveals to us God's working through history, his character, and how to follow him. In all of these ways, we are drawn to God and experience a stronger connection with him.

Returning full circle, another way of connecting with God is through the study of and reflection on the cosmos. Even though we can obtain a much better understanding of the character of God through the person of Jesus Christ as revealed in Scripture, there is still something about the mystery and awe of the cosmos that calls us back and connects us with God. As we scale the heights of new discoveries and launch out to new worlds, something about the unveiling of the unknown of the universe brings us to see the fingerprint of God. "The heavens speak of the Creator's glory, and the skies proclaim the work of his hands. Day after day they pour forth speech; night after night they display his knowledge" (Ps 19:1-2).

I conclude with this poem:

Between

Between the visible and the invisible,
Between the brightest stars and darkest night,
We sense a glimpse of truth, a ray of light.

Between the black holes and anti-matter,
Between the provable and the unknown,
Deep within ourselves, we groan.

Between the mighty Orion and beautiful Pleiades,
What can we really know, what can we surmise?
From across the cosmos, our hearts arise.

Behind us our world is crumbling,
Ahead of us, it is so unsure;
Yet our heart cries out, to find a cure.

Between scientific fact and biblical truths;
We stand on the precipice between faith and doubt,
Ready to jump, we give a shout.

Between the infinite and the finite,
We see the Son, a glimpse of thin-space.
We reach out to him, and touch his face.

—Merlin Merritt

Notes

1. David Atkinson, *The Message of Genesis 1-11* (Leicester, England: Intervarsity Press, 1990) 27.

2. John David Weaver, *In the Beginning God* (Oxford UK: Regents Park College, with Smyth & Helwys Publishing, Inc., Macon GA, 1994) 29.

3. James W. Fowler, *Stages of Faith, The Psychology of Human Development and the Quest for Meaning* (New York: Harper Collins, 1995) 185.

4. John Francis Xavier O'Conor, *A Study of Francis Thompson's Hound of Heaven* (New York: John Lane Co., 1912) 7.

Other available titles from

#Connect
Reaching Youth Across the Digital Divide
Brian Foreman

Reaching our youth across the digital divide is a struggle for parents, ministers, and other adults who work with Generation Z—today's teenagers. *#Connect* leads readers into the technological landscape, encourages conversations with teenagers, and reminds us all to be the presence of Christ in every facet of our lives. 978-1-57312-693-9 120 pages/pb **$13.00**

Atonement in the Apocalypse
An Exposé of the Defeat of Evil
Robert W. Canoy

Revelation calls believers to see themselves through the unique lens of redemptive atonement and to live and model daily that they see themselves in the present moment as redeemed people. Having thus seen themselves, believers likewise are directed to see and to relate to others in this world the very way that God has seen them from eternity.

978-1-57312-946-6 218 pages/pb **$22.00**

Beginnings
A Reverend and a Rabbi Talk About the Stories of Genesis
Michael Smith and Rami Shapiro

Editor Aaron Herschel Shapiro declares that stories "must be retold—not just repeated, but reinvented, reimagined, and reexperienced" to remain vital in the world. Mike and Rami continue their conversations from the *Mount and Mountain* books, exploring the places where their traditions intersect and diverge, listening to each other as they respond to the stories of Genesis. 978-1-57312-772-1 202 pages/pb **$18.00**

Bugles in the Afternoon
Dealing with Discouragement and Disillusionment in Ministry
Judson Edwards

In *Bugles in the Afternoon*, Edwards writes, "My long experience in the church has convinced me that most ministers—both professional and lay—spend time under the juniper tree. Those ministers who have served more than ten years and not been depressed, discouraged, or disillusioned can hold their annual convention in a phone booth."

978-1-57312-865-0 148 pages/pb **$16.00**

To order call **1-800-747-3016** or visit **www.helwys.com**

A Christian's Guide to Islam
Michael D. McCullar

A Christian's Guide to Islam provides a brief but accurate guide to Muslim formation, history, structure, beliefs, practices, and goals. It explores to what degree the tenets of Islam have been misinterpreted, corrupted, or abused over the centuries.

978-1-57312-512-3 128 pages/pb **$16.00**

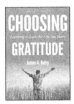
Choosing Gratitude
Learning to Love the Life You Have
James A. Autry

Autry reminds us that gratitude is a choice, a spiritual—not social—process. He suggests that if we cultivate gratitude as a way of being, we may not change the world and its ills, but we can change our response to the world. If we fill our lives with moments of gratitude, we will indeed love the life we have.

978-1-57312-614-4 144 pages/pb **$15.00**

Choosing Gratitude 365 Days a Year
Your Daily Guide to Grateful Living
James A. Autry and Sally J. Pederson

Filled with quotes, poems, and the inspired voices of both Pederson and Autry, in a society consumed by fears of not having "enough"—money, possessions, security, and so on—this book suggests that if we cultivate gratitude as a way of being, we may not change the world and its ills, but we can change our response to the world.

978-1-57312-689-2 210 pages/pb **$18.00**

Countercultural Worship
A Plea to Evangelicals in a Secular Age
Mark G. McKim

Evangelical worship, McKim argues, has drifted far from both its biblical roots and historic origins, leaving evangelicals in danger of becoming mere chaplains to the wider culture, oblivious to the contradictions between what the secular culture says is real and important and what Scripture says is real and important.

978-1-57312-873-5 174 pages/pb **$19.00**

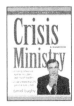
Crisis Ministry: A Handbook
Daniel G. Bagby

Covering more than 25 crisis pastoral care situations, this book provides a brief, practical guide for church leaders and other caregivers responding to stressful situations in the lives of parishioners. It tells how to resource caregiving professionals in the community who can help people in distress.

978-1-57312-370-9 154 pages/pb **$15.00**

To order call 1-800-747-3016 or visit www.helwys.com

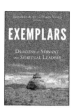
Exemplars
Deacons as Servant and Spiritual Leaders
Elizabeth Allen and Daniel Vestal, eds.

Who Do Deacons Need to Be? What Do Deacons Need to Know? What Do Deacons Need to Do? These three questions form the basis for *Exemplars: Deacons as Servant and Spiritual Leaders*. They are designed to encourage robust conversation within diaconates as well as between deacons, clergy, and other laity. *978-1-57312-876-6 128 pages/pb* **$15.00**

The Exile and Beyond (All the Bible series)
Wayne Ballard

The *Exile and Beyond* brings to life the sacred literature of Israel and Judah that comprises the exilic and postexilic communities of faith. It covers Ezekiel, Isaiah, Haggai, Zechariah, Malachi, 1 & 2 Chronicles, Ezra, Nehemiah, Joel, Jonah, Song of Songs, Esther, and Daniel. *978-1-57312-759-2 196 pages/pb* **$16.00**

Fierce Love
Desperate Measures for Desperate Times
Jeanie Miley

Fierce Love is about learning to see yourself and know yourself as a conduit of love, operating from a full heart instead of trying to find someone to whom you can hook up your emotional hose and fill up your empty heart. *978-1-57312-810-0 276 pages/pb* **$18.00**

Five Hundred Miles
Reflections on Calling and Pilgrimage
Lauren Brewer Bass

Spain's Camino de Santiago, the Way of St. James, has been a cherished pilgrimage path for centuries, visited by countless people searching for healing, solace, purpose, and hope. These stories from her five-hundred-mile-walk is Lauren Brewer Bass's honest look at the often winding, always surprising journey of a calling. *978-1-57312-812-4 142 pages/pb* **$16.00**

A Five-Mile Walk
Exploring Themes in the Experience of Christian Faith and Discipleship
Michael B. Brown

Sometimes the Christian journey is a stroll along quiet shores. Other times it is an uphill climb on narrow, snow-covered mountain paths. Usually, it is simply walking in the direction of wholeness, one step after another, sometimes even two steps forward and one step back.

978-1-57312-852-0 196 pages/pb **$18.00**

To order call 1-800-747-3016 or visit www.helwys.com

Glimpses from State Street
Wayne Ballard

As a collection of devotionals, Glimpses from State Street provides a wealth of insights and new ways to consider and develop our fellowship with Christ. It also serves as a window into the relationship between a small town pastor and a welcoming congregation.

978-1-57312-841-4 158 pages/pb **$15.00**

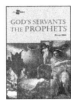
God's Servants, the Prophets
Bryan Bibb

God's Servants, the Prophets covers the Israelite and Judean prophetic literature from the preexilic period. It includes Amos, Hosea, Isaiah, Micah, Zephaniah, Nahum, Habakkuk, Jeremiah, and Obadiah.

978-1-57312-758-5 208 pages/pb **$16.00**

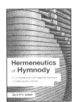
Hermeneutics of Hymnody
A Comprehensive and Integrated Approach to Understanding Hymns
Scotty Gray

Scotty Gray's Hermeneutics of Hymnody is a comprehensive and integrated approach to understanding hymns. It is unique in its holistic and interrelated exploration of seven of the broad facets of this most basic forms of Christian literature. A chapter is devoted to each and relates that facet to all of the others.

978-157312-767-7 432 pages/pb **$28.00**

Holy Hilarity
A Funny Study of Genesis
Mark Roncace

In this fun, meaningful, and practical study of Genesis, Mark Roncace brings readers fifty-three short chapters of wit and amusing observations about the biblical stories, followed by five thought-provoking questions for individual reflection or group discussion. Humorous, yet reverent, this refreshing approach to Bible study invites us, whatever our background, to wrestle with the issues in the text and discover the ways those issues intersect our own messy lives. It's seriously entertaining.

978-157312-892-6 230 pages/pb **$17.00**

If Jesus Isn't the Answer . . . He Sure Asks the Right Questions!
J. Daniel Day

Taking eleven of Jesus' questions as its core, Day invites readers into their own conversation with Jesus. Equal parts testimony, theological instruction, pastoral counseling, and autobiography, the book is ultimately an invitation to honest Christian discipleship.

978-1-57312-797-4 148 pages/pb **$16.00**

To order call **1-800-747-3016** or visit **www.helwys.com**

Jonah (Annual Bible Study series)
Reluctant Prophet, Merciful God

Taylor Sandlin

The book of Jonah invites readers to ask important questions about who God is and who God calls us to be in response. Along with the prophet, we ask questions such as What kind of God is the God of Israel? and Who falls within the sphere of God's care? Most importantly, perhaps, we find ourselves asking How will I respond when I discover that God loves the people I love to hate? These sessions invite readers to wrestle with these questions and others like them as we discover God's mercy for both the worst of sinners and the most reluctant of prophets.

Teaching Guide 978-1-57312-910-7 164 pages/pb **$14.00**
Study Guide 978-1-57312-911-4 96 pages/pb **$6.00**

Judaism
A Brief Guide to Faith and Practice

Sharon Pace

Sharon Pace's newest book is a sensitive and comprehensive introduction to Judaism. How does belief in the One God and a universal morality shape the way in which Jews see the world? How does one find meaning in life and the courage to endure suffering? How does one mark joy and forge community ties?

978-1-57312-644-1 144 pages/pb **$16.00**

Live the Stories
50 Interactive Children's Sermons

Andrew Noe

Live the Stories provides church leaders a practical guide to teaching children during the worship service through play—and invites the rest of the congregation to join the fun. Noe's lessons allow children to play, laugh, and act out the stories of our faith and turn the sanctuary into a living testimony to what God has done in the past, is doing in the present, and will do in the future. As they learn the stories and grow, our children will develop in their faith.

978-1-57312-943-5 128 pages/pb **$14.00**

Loyal Dissenters
Reading Scripture and Talking Freedom with 17th-century English Baptists

Lee Canipe

When Baptists in 17th-century England wanted to talk about freedom, they unfailingly began by reading the Bible—and what they found in Scripture inspired their compelling (and, ultimately, successful) arguments for religious liberty. In an age of widespread anxiety, suspicion, and hostility, these early Baptists refused to worship God in keeping with the king's command.

978-1-57312-872-8 178 pages/pb **$19.00**

To order call 1-800-747-3016 or visit www.helwys.com

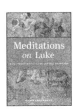
Meditations on Luke
Daily Devotions from the Gentile Physician
Chris Cadenhead

Readers searching for a fresh encounter with Scripture can delve into *Meditations on Luke*, a collection of daily devotions intended to guide the reader through the book of Luke, which gives us some of the most memorable stories in all of Scripture. The Scripture, response, and prayer will guide readers' own meditations as they listen and respond to God's voice, coming to us through Luke's Gospel.

978-1-57312-947-3 328 pages/pb **$22.00**

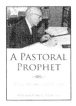
A Pastoral Prophet
Sermons and Prayers of Wayne E. Oates
William Powell Tuck, ed.

Read these sermons and prayers and look directly into the heart of Wayne Oates. He was a consummate counselor, theologian, and writer, but first of all he was a pastor. . . . He gave voice to our deepest hurts, then followed with words we long to hear: you are not alone.

—Kay Shurden
Associate Professor Emeritus, Clinical Education,
Mercer University School of Medicine, Macon, Georgia

978-157312-955-8 160 pages/pb **$18.00**

Place Value
The Journey to Where You Are
Katie Sciba

Does a place have value? Can a place change us? Is it possible for God to use the place you are in to form you? From Victoria, Texas to Indonesia, Belize, Australia, and beyond, Katie Sciba's wanderlust serves as a framework to understand your own places of deep emotion and how God may have been weaving redemption around you all along.

978-157312-829-2 138 pages/pb **$15.00**

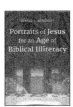
Portraits of Jesus
for an Age of Biblical Illiteracy
Gerald L. Borchert

Despite our era of communication and information overload, biblical illiteracy is widespread. In *Portraits of Jesus*, Gerald L. Borchert assists both ministers and laypeople with a return to what the New Testament writers say about this stunning Jesus who shocked the world and called a small company of believers into an electrifying transformation.

978-157312-940-4 212 pages/pb **$20.00**

To order call **1-800-747-3016** or visit **www.helwys.com**

Preaching that Connects
Charles B. Bugg and Alan Redditt

How does the minister stay focused on the holy when the daily demands of the church seem relentless? How do we come to a preaching event with a sense that God is working in us and through us? In *Preaching that Connects*, Charles Bugg and Alan Redditt explore the balancing act of a minister's authority as preacher, sharing what the congregation needs to hear, and the communal role as pastor, listening to God alongside congregants. 978-157312-887-2 128 pages/pb **$15.00**

Reading Isaiah
(Reading the Old Testament series)
A Literary and Theological Commentary
Hyun Chul Paul Kim

While closely exegeting key issues of each chapter, this commentary also explores interpretive relevance and significance between ancient texts and the modern world. Engaging with theological messages of the book of Isaiah as a unified whole, the commentary will both illuminate and inspire readers to wrestle with its theological implications for today's church and society.

978-1-57312-925-1 352 pages/pb **$33.00**

Reading Jeremiah
(Reading the Old Testament series)
A Literary and Theological Commentary
Corrine Carvalho

Reflecting the ways that communal tragedy permeates communal identity, the book of Jeremiah as literary text embodies the confusion, disorientation, and search for meaning that all such tragedy elicits. Just as the fall of Jerusalem fractured the Judean community and undercut every foundation on which it built its identity, so too the book itself (or more properly, the scroll) jumbles images, genres, and perspectives. 978-1-57312-924-4 186 pages/pb **$32.00**

Ruth & Esther (Smyth & Helwys Bible Commentary)
Kandy Queen-Sutherland

Ruth and Esther are the only two women for whom books of the Hebrew Bible are named. This distinction in itself sets the books apart from other biblical texts that bear male names, address the community through its male members, recall the workings of God and human history through a predominately male perspective, and look to the future through male heirs. These books are particularly stories of survival. The story of Ruth focuses on the survival of a family; Esther focuses on the survival of a people. 978-1-57312-891-9 544 pages/hc **$60.00**

To order call **1-800-747-3016** or visit **www.helwys.com**

Sessions with Psalms (Sessions Bible Studies series)
Prayers for All Seasons
Eric and Alicia D. Porterfield

Useful to seminar leaders during preparation and group discussion, as well as in individual Bible study, Sessions with Psalms is a ten-session study designed to explore what it looks like for the words of the psalms to become the words of our prayers. Each session is followed by a thought-provoking page of questions. 978-1-57312-768-4 136 pages/pb **$14.00**

Sessions with Isaiah (Sessions Bible Studies series)
What to Do When the World Caves In
James M. King

The book of Isaiah begins in the years of national stress when, under various kings, Israel was surrounded by more powerful neighbors and foolishly sought foreign alliances rather than dependence on Yahweh. It continues with the natural result of that unfaithfulness: conquest by the great power in the region, Babylon, and the captivity of many of Israel's best and brightest in that foreign land. The book concludes anticipating their return to the land of promise and strong admonitions about the people's conduct—but we also hear God's reassuring messages of comfort and restoration, offered to all who repent.

978-1-57312-942-8 130 pages/pb **$14.00**

Stained-Glass Millennials
Rob Lee

We've heard the narrative that millennials are done with the institutional church; they've packed up and left. This book is an alternative to that story and chronicles the journey of millennials who are investing their lives in the institution because they believe in the church's resurrecting power. Through anecdotes and interviews, Rob Lee takes readers on a journey toward God's unfolding future for the church, a beloved institution in desperate need of change. 978-1-57312-926-8 156 pages/pb **$16.00**

Star Thrower
A Pastor's Handbook
William Powell Tuck

In *Star Thrower: A Pastor's Handbook*, William Powell Tuck draws on over fifty years of experience to share his perspective on being an effective pastor. He describes techniques for sermon preparation, pastoral care, and church administration, as well as for conducting Communion, funeral, wedding, and baptismal services. He also includes advice for working with laity and church staff, coping with church conflict, and nurturing one's own spiritual and family life. 978-1-57312-889-6 244 pages/pb **$15.00**

To order call **1-800-747-3016** or visit **www.helwys.com**

Tell the Truth, Shame the Devil
Stories about the Challenges of Young Pastors
James Elllis III, ed.

A pastor's life is uniquely difficult. *Tell the Truth, Shame the Devil*, then, is an attempt to expose some of the challenges that young clergy often face. While not exhaustive, this collection of essays is a superbly compelling and diverse introduction to how tough being a pastor under the age of thirty-five can be.   978-1-57312-839-1   198 pages/pb   **$18.00**

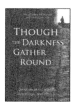

Though the Darkness Gather Round
Devotions about Infertility, Miscarriage, and Infant Loss
Mary Elizabeth Hill Hanchey and Erin McClain, eds.

Much courage is required to weather the long grief of infertility and the sudden grief of miscarriage and infant loss. This collection of devotions by men and women, ministers, chaplains, and lay leaders who can speak of such sorrow, is a much-needed resource and precious gift for families on this journey and the faith communities that walk beside them.

    978-1-57312-811-7   180 pages/pb   **$19.00**

Time for Supper
Invitations to Christ's Table
Brett Younger

Some scholars suggest that every meal in literature is a communion scene. Could every meal in the Bible be a communion text? Could every passage be an invitation to God's grace? These meditations on the Lord's Supper help us listen to the myriad of ways God invites us to gratefully, reverently, and joyfully share the cup of Christ.   978-1-57312-720-2   246 pages/pb   **$18.00**

A True Hope
Jedi Perils and the Way of Jesus
Joshua Hays

Star Wars offers an accessible starting point for considering substantive issues of faith, philosophy, and ethics. In *A True Hope*, Joshua Hays explores some of these challenging ideas through the sayings of the Jedi Masters, examining the ways the worldview of the Jedi is at odds with that of the Bible.   978-1-57312-770-7   186 pages/pb   **$18.00**

To order call **1-800-747-3016** or visit **www.helwys.com**

Clarence Jordan's Cotton Patch Gospel

The Complete Collection

Hardback • 448 pages
Retail 50.00 • Your Price 25.00

Paperback • 448 pages
Retail 40.00 • Your Price 20.00

The Cotton Patch Gospel, by Koinonia Farm founder Clarence Jordan, recasts the stories of Jesus and the letters of the New Testament into the language and culture of the mid-twentieth-century South. Born out of the civil rights struggle, these now-classic translations of much of the New Testament bring the far-away places of Scripture closer to home: Gainesville, Selma, Birmingham, Atlanta, Washington D.C.

More than a translation, *The Cotton Patch Gospel* continues to make clear the startling relevance of Scripture for today. Now for the first time collected in a single, hardcover volume, this edition comes complete with a new Introduction by President Jimmy Carter, a Foreword by Will D. Campbell, and an Afterword by Tony Campolo. Smyth & Helwys Publishing is proud to help reintroduce these seminal works of Clarence Jordan to a new generation of believers, in an edition that can be passed down to generations still to come.

To order call **1-800-747-3016**
or visit **www.helwys.com**

Printed in Great Britain
by Amazon